EDUCATING THE 1
HAS BEEN ANNOUNC
IN THE ERIC DATABASE

As a result of its acceptance by ERIC, an earlier, abridged edition of *Educating the Entire Person* can now be found in the microfiche collections of 891 major libraries worldwide; and a summary of the book is available for retrieval internationally from ERIC's widely accessible online database. Its locating number in the ERIC database is: ED 369 523. (ERIC disseminates educational materials it deems "timely and significant to the educational community.")

PRAISE FOR
EDUCATING THE ENTIRE PERSON

The following prominent American educators and psychologists have praised *Educating the Entire Person.* Some of their endorsements apply to earlier editions of the book, which were published in 1993 and 1994.

1. "I have just finished reading your *Educating the Entire Person,* and I am inspired by the power and clarity of its message. I think that you have done a most creative job of incorporating the best of modern thinking about learning and moving it forward into a new dimension. A special contribution I think you have made is the integration of lifelong learning with the education of children and youth. As I see it, this little book will be helpful to both teachers/mentors/facilitators/parents (the learning resource providers) and learners. I hope that it reaches them all."
- Dr. Malcolm Knowles, Professor Emeritus of Adult Education
North Carolina State University

2. "In this era of educational turmoil, it is a pleasure to read a sensible prescription. *Educating the Entire Person* faces the difficulties inherent in the educational process and proposes a radically different model of learning that has an excellent chance of confronting the current crisis and transforming it into an opportunity. Our children's future depends upon a change of this nature, and Ron Dultz has

constructed an original approach to the morass of problems that teachers face daily in their classrooms."

-Dr. Stanley Krippner, Professor of Psychology,
Saybrook Institute

3. "I would like to see some educational schools and groups experiment with your suggestions, to see how they actually work out."

-Dr. Albert Ellis, Psychologist,
Institute for Rational-Emotive Therapy

4. "You have written a very intelligent book. It is thoughtful, well-organized and easy to read and understand."

-Dr. James Comer, Professor of Psychiatry,
Yale University Child Study Center

5. "I believe that your ideas in *Educating the Entire Person* are generally well founded."

-Dr. Wilbert McKeachie, Professor of Psychology,
University of Michigan

6. "Perhaps the major contribution of this paperback lies in its inclination to ask readers to think anew, divergently and flexibly, about certain dimensions of the whole person and his learning."

-Dr. M. Dale Baughman, Professor Emeritus of Education,
Indiana State University

7. "*Educating the Entire Person* is a noteworthy effort to recover for the child spontaneity, meaning, and joy in learning."

-Dr. Maurice Friedman, Professor Emeritus of Philosophy,
San Diego State University

EDUCATING THE ENTIRE PERSON

by RON DULTZ

Published by:
Ron Dultz Publishing
P.O. Box 370985
Reseda, CA 91337

Manufactured in the United States of America

Library of Congress catalog card number: 78-52911

ISBN 0-9601636-0-3

Note:

Some students who critiqued the 1994 edition of *Educating the Entire Person* complained about my use of male pronouns exclusively even though I explained at the beginning of the book that the reasons for it were to maintain clarity and economy of style, and because the English language does not provide dual-gender pronouns (pronouns which can be used to signify both male and female simultaneously). Although I have tried to address the problem in this edition by using more female pronouns, there appears to be no completely satisfactory solution to the problem short of creating dual-gender pronouns in the English language.

One solution is to use he/she, him/her, his/her, himself/herself in all instances in which a dual-gender pronoun is called for; but upon trying to do so, I found that it results in very clumsy prose, disrupts the flow of the piece and even interferes with comprehension. In one eleven-line paragraph in my essay entitled "The Independent Teacher," I found sixteen instances in which the use of dual-gender pronouns would be applicable; and when I tried to use he/she, him/her, his/her where applicable, the clarity and flow of the paragraph suffered substantially.

To more fairly distribute male and female pronouns in this edition, I have decided to use mostly female pronouns when referring to the teacher and mostly male pronouns when referring to the student, admittedly not a perfect solution; however, it is worth noting that, in her writings, Maria Montessori used male pronouns when referring to the student and female pronouns when referring to the teacher.

It is worth mentioning that the acting profession now favors usage of the word actor when referring to both male and female performers; whereas, in previous decades, the word actress was commonly used.

– the author

CONTENTS

FOREWORD

Educating the Entire Person is not the usual kind of text-book on personality and education. It is more than that. Despite its brevity, it gets at the very heart of the problems of educating the whole person – the critical objectives of such education are outlined and the means whereby these objectives can best be achieved are proposed. It offers a different perspective on the entire process.

The author acknowledges the importance of having a broad range of factual knowledge. However, he considers other objectives more important. He would make sure that "each individual develops naturally, in accordance with his abilities, inclinations, needs and growth patterns." He would also equip them with the skills to be self-sufficient financially. He would give attention to moral development and the development of a clear, precise and satisfactory identity of one's own.

The author maintains that the key to achieving these objectives is through developing and using individual and classroom learning profiles. Learning profiles consist of the individual's and classroom's needs, interests and inclinations. It is only by being faithful to them that a genuine love for learning can be nurtured.

Some readers will disagree with some of the ideas in *Educating the Entire Person*, and this is alright. The best decisions occur when there is a tolerance for disagreement. Original ideas are at first suspect, and are too frequently ignored or ridiculed instead of questioned and considered. I think the original ideas in the book are worth questioning and considering. They need to be viewed in different perspectives.

The author also offers original ideas about such matters as: mandatory learning, unlearning and reevaluating, moving the whole person forward, the right to choose the subject matter to be learned, getting a total view, the reaction process, speaking out, and motivating one's self to learn. It will be a challenge to consider and test these ideas.

When I was Director of the Bureau of Educational Research at the University of Minnesota, the Dean challenged the faculty of the College of Education every fall. He would say, "Half of what you are teaching is false and it is time for you to find out which half this is." There was within the College of Education a great deal of disagreement, but there was also tolerance for disagreement. This same Dean told me when I was hired that he wanted me to teach one course. It didn't matter to him what course I taught, but he wanted me to make this course famous. I taught a course entitled "Personality and Mental Health" for eight years, and it did become famous. Students from almost every discipline were attracted to it – from art, drama, speech therapy, counseling, psychology, nursing, elementary and secondary education, vocational education, school psychology, higher education, special education, gifted education and social work.

I wish that I had had something like *Educating the Entire Person* before I began. I discovered some of the same ideas in teaching the course as in reading the book, as well as some others. It was exciting and rewarding. Ron Dultz's idea of unlearning and reevaluating would have been useful to me and the others challenged by the Minnesota Dean to find out what false information they had been teaching. I hope that the readers of *Educating the Entire Person* will be challenged. I assure you that accepting this challenge will be exciting and rewarding.

E. Paul Torrance*
Athens, Georgia, March 1997

*Dr. E. Paul Torrance was appointed by the President of the United States to be Forum Chairman of the Early Childhood Group of the White House Conference on Children in 1970.

He was chairman of the department of educational psychology at the University of Georgia from 1966-1978.

In 1978, he was cited by Phi Delta Kappa as one of 10 top contributors of significant research in the United States and Canada, and by the Institution of Scientific Information as one of 100 most cited social scientists.

He has published 1,500 articles and 35 books. His awards and honors, which are too numerous to list, continue to accumulate as of the printing of this book.

INTRODUCTION

The human mind exhibits magnificent qualities and capabilities. If properly nurtured and developed, it will be a reliable helpmate throughout a person's lifetime, and a good guide through the difficult terrain of life. And, when properly influenced by the various principles of morality throughout its developing years, it will be inspired to perform for the sake of what is wholesome, honorable, good and decent in life. But the human mind is also vulnerable and delicate. It is susceptible to many things, and can be harmed in many ways. Its development can be hindered, undermined and obstructed. Its growth into an instrument capable of efficient reasoning, wise decisions and sound judgment can be derailed.

The type of learning that a particular mind undergoes, and the type of teaching it is exposed to, are essential factors in determining if it will fulfill its potential, stagnate, or develop improperly. Those who naively believe that learning always occurs for the betterment of the student should be reminded that brainwashing and indoctrination are forms of learning. A mind that is brainwashed into thinking a certain way, or that is indoctrinated with certain points of view, is a fanatical and prejudiced mind. It has not used reasoning and logic to arrive at what it knows, and so it cannot be expected to use reasoning and logic in applying or implementing the information and knowledge that it has. Such a mind is dangerous. In like fashion, learning that occurs because it is expected of students, or because students feel pressured to learn, should not be expected to be suited to their learning needs. And methods of teaching that do not focus on the specific learning needs of students should not be expected to have a beneficial affect upon them. When learning occurs simply because it is required of a student or expected of him, much of what is learned is, at best, excess and cumbersome baggage in the student's life. But, more often, such learning is an assault upon his happiness, peace of mind, spontaneity and free spirit. More often, it violates his integrity, invades and undermines his identity and individuality. More often, it derails the delicate, natural process of the development of the self that is unique to each individual.

Unfortunately, the rights and needs of the student have been poorly represented by most who have formulated educational theories and policies in the past, and their errors have been

11

adopted by a majority of teachers. The learning and teaching that are occurring in our schools are often unhealthy and dangerous. The human mind was never meant to be a passive receiver of facts and information, which have been arbitrarily gathered by others, and just as arbitrarily foisted upon it. Being subjected to a steady diet of focusing on subject matter at the request of others, and following learning procedures designed by others, is not appropriate to the delicate and intensely individualistic nature of the human mind. A far different approach to learning and teaching must be formulated, and then properly applied, if responsible teaching and effective learning are to take place. This book attempts to provide a philosophical foundation for productive learning and responsible teaching.

Ron Dultz July 1,1993

SECOND INTRODUCTION

Educating the Entire Person now has a history and I, its author, am a lot more savvy since having written the earlier editions. In preparation for printing this expanded version of the book, it is appropriate that I write an updated introduction to satisfy some of the concerns and questions of the many college students from whom I have received feedback about the book, and to provide a more appropriate overview for understanding and evaluating the text.

Reviews

Educating the Entire Person has now received two major reviews within academic literature in the professions of education and psychology.

One is an extremely favorable review by Dr. Malcolm Knowles, who is referred to in the ERIC database as "the father of adult learning theory." His review of *Educating the Entire Person* appears in the July/August '95 issue of *Adult Learning* (pp. 6 & 31), which is published by the American Association for Adult & Continuing Education. By coincidence, a video about Malcolm Knowles is also reviewed on page 6 of the same issue, in which Malcolm Knowles is referred to by the reviewer as "one of the few living icons in the field of adult education." In his review of *Educating the Entire Person*, Dr. Knowles said, " .... Ron Dultz makes a powerful case for transforming our entire educational system – elementary, secondary, higher and adult – away from the traditional teacher controlled, information transmitting, and recall-testing lock-step process we have all experienced in our previous schooling to what Paulo Freire and I would call a learner-empowering system. .... While Dultz addresses his book primarily to the teachers of children and youth, its basic principles, methods and spirit apply to adult learners and their teachers, mentors, supervisors, and peer helpers as well. I wish I had had this book to inspire and guide me when I started teaching adults."

The second major review is by the prominent psychologist, Dr. Albert Ellis. It appeared in the June '96 issue of the American Psychological Association's book review journal, *Contemporary Psychology*. Although a mixed review, it ends quite positively with the words, " .... Dultz presents a number of interesting and at times fascinating hypotheses that can merit considerable evaluation and experimentation." Dr. Ellis and I afterward debated his review of *Educating the Entire Person* in the Feb. '97 issue of *Contemporary Psychology* (pp. 175-176).

A Note on the Format

Educating the Entire Person is composed of a collection of separate essays. The essays do not always follow each other in a logical sequence, but they are all essential and relevant parts of a complex philosophy of education I am trying to communicate to the reader. Some of the essays apply to the education of youth, others to the education of adults, while others are applicable to both.

Use of this Book

Educators, students and the general public will decide how to use this book, but I believe it is worthwhile to know the uses for which I designed the book:

1. As a theory in support of voluntary, self-directed learning for youngsters.

2. As a theory to enhance the self-development of all students and learners. I maintain that learning for self-development is the foremost purpose of education, and that a lot of the educating that occurs in our schools is harmful to students because it interferes with their proper self-development. (For an analysis of some of the problems and challenges of understanding and developing one's self, please see my essay entitled "Understanding One's Self," published in my book entitled *A New Approach to Human Psychology*.)

3. As a theory which points out that what educators demand of their students often seriously conflicts with their students' personal needs; and, as a result, harms the students instead of benefiting them.

4. As a theory around which the general public can coalesce in better understanding the educational process and in improving our schools.

Theorists and Schools I Endorse

The educational theorists with whom I concur are: Leo

14

Tolstoy and John Holt. Three existing schools whose educational methods I agree with are: Sudbury Valley School, Framingham, MA; Windsor House Public School, Vancouver, British Columbia, Canada; Summerhill School, Suffolk, England. My comments on these theorists and schools can be found in the Feb. '97 issue of *Contemporary Psychology* (pp. 175-176) A portion of those comments, in which I quote two of the world's greatest educators, cannot be said often enough, and I shall duplicate them here:

In his newsletters about Yasnaya Polyana[1], the successful experimental school for youngsters Leo Tolstoy directed for three years on his estate in Russia, he stated, "the person being educated must have the full power to express his dissatisfaction with, or at least to withdraw from, that part of his education which does not satisfy his instinct." Even though his school was lesson-based, meaning that he and the teachers he hired gave lessons on various subjects on a daily basis,"the pupil always had the right not to go to school and even, when he came, not to listen to the teacher." Tolstoy believed in "leaving the students complete freedom to learn and conduct their affairs as they wish." To insure that students' rights were respected,"no student was obliged to remember today any lesson or anything that was done yesterday."

In John Holt's books[2], he made the following comments with regard to the education of youngsters:"Uninvited teaching does not make learning. For the most part, such teaching prevents learning. .... The school should be a great smorgasbord of intellectual, creative and athletic activities, from which each child could take whatever he wanted, and as much as he wanted, or as little. .... What is essential is to realize that children learn independently, not in bunches; that they learn out of interest and curiosity, not to appease the adults in power; and that they ought to be in control of their own learning, deciding for themselves what they want to learn and how they want to learn it. .... We can best help children learn, not by deciding what we think they should learn and thinking of ingenious ways to teach it to them, but by making the world, as far as we can, accessible to them, paying serious attention to what they do, answering their questions – if they have any – and helping them explore the things they are most interested in."

References

[1]Pinch, A. & Armstrong, M. (1982). *Tolstoy on Education* (pp. 84, 89, 92, 95). East Brunswick NJ: Associated University Presses – Fairleigh Dickinson University Press.

15

[2]Holt, John (1989). *Learning All the Time* (pp. 128, 162). Reading, MA: Addison-Wesley Publishing Co.

Holt, John (1995). *How Children Fail* (p. 295). Reading, MA: Addison-Wesley Publishing Co.

Holt, John (1995). *How Children Learn* (p. 290). Reading, MA: Addison-Wesley Publishing Co.

Unschoolers

Home schooling is now legal in the U.S. in all fifty states, and it is growing in popularity within the U.S. and around the world. Hundreds of thousands of children are being home schooled in the U.S. alone. Unschoolers are a popular branch of the homeschooling movement, and they are a group whose theories and practices I agree with and wholeheartedly endorse. Unschoolers believe, and have proven, that youngsters can learn effectively without being subjected to any *mandatory or required curriculum, tests or assignments*. There is a separate section in this book about unschoolers.

Student Critiques

The 1994 edition of *Educating the Entire Person* (pp.11-12 & pp. 27-135 of this new edition) has been critiqued by nearly one thousand college students studying in the graduate and undergraduate departments of Education and Psychology at more than twenty-five colleges in twenty states. It is clear from these critiques that college students are much aroused by the contents of the book and have a love/hate response to the book. Many students love the book, many are vehemently opposed to it, and many love parts of the book and are vehemently opposed to other parts of it. I believe the polarity of the responses is due to the difficulty and complexity of the overall topic addressed in the book, and due to the fact that most students are reared in traditional ways of thinking about education and practicing it. A number of the professors who used the book commented that it was excellent for stimulating meaningful debate among students, and as a thinking-skills exercise.

Perhaps the most important discovery which the college student critiques of *Educating the Entire Person* has yielded is the fact that the idea of a system of educating youngsters based upon voluntary learning, without any *mandatory curricula, tests or assignments,* is rarely taught in our colleges. I know this because, of the approximately one thousand critiques I received from students at over twenty-five colleges scattered across the U.S., only a very small percentage had previously entertained the idea of non-compulsory education for youth, and almost none had conceived of non-compulsory education for youth as a viable system which could be undertaken on a large scale once understood and vigorously advocated by sufficient proponents of the idea.

Here is a brief sampling of the many positive responses the 1994 edition of *Educating the Entire Person* (pp. 11-12 & pp. 27-135 of this new edition) received from college students:

1. "I like the book very much. It doesn't read like the usual, boring textbooks we are so often assigned."– student, UEDUC 3350.02, Lesley College, Cambridge, MA.

2. "*Educating the Entire Person* was an inspiring book about how to teach children to learn what is important in becoming an integrated person. .... Seeing this theory used in a school where the entire school was engaged would be helpful. .... I would love to teach in such a school ...." – student, ECPY 512-30, University of Louisville, Louisville, KY.

3. "I found the book to be very interesting and informative. Many of its ideas were things I had never thought about. This book would be very beneficial to persons of all careers." – graduate student, college of education and counseling, South Dakota State University.

4. "Overall, the book did present a new approach to the educational system. This approach is described in a thorough and intelligent manner. It is my opinion that some of these methods should be utilized to help the failing system."– graduate student, college teaching course, Florida Atlantic University.

5. "The book provides different ways of looking at the educational process of today. Mr. Dultz discusses and explains alternatives and/or solutions to the educational problems facing both student and teacher alike. It is my recommendation that undergraduate students read this book." – Ed.D. student, the University of West Florida.

6. "The content was thought provoking and is excellent reading for educators and new parents" – Ed.D. student, Delta State University, Cleveland, Mississippi.

7. "Ron Dultz speaks in terms that are understandable and challenges the reader to think in new, innovative ways. I would

recommend this book to many people, despite what their occupation may be." – student, Education 253, Columbia College, Columbia, SC.

8. "*Educating the Entire Person* may be the answer to the current era of educational turmoil. I myself would like to see further research in this area being done." – student, Education 4700, Kansas Newman College, Wichita, KS.

9. "*Educating the Entire Person* is an excellent guide for the upcoming teacher. Mr. Dultz gives us a new and innovative way of educating our children in the classroom. He gives us a good message on how we as teachers can better assist children in learning and how we can facilitate their environments so they can get the most out of their education." – student, Psychology 3,000, Appalachian State University, Boone, NC.

10. "*Educating the Entire Person* delivers a wonderful dream. .... We have been discussing many learning theories including those of Albert Bandura, Reuven Feuerstein, Howard Gardner, Lev Vygotsky and Matthew Lippman. Your book reflects many of the great ideas from these heralded theorists. I wish I had a dozen teachers utilizing its philosophy, it would have made my life better. In addition to being required reading for future teachers, this book should be part of every adult's guide to parenting." – student, Education 315, Westminster College, Salt Lake City, UT.

11. "Each chapter was very educational because they all gave me an outlook as to how I can become a better teacher in the future." – student, educational psychology class, Northern Illinois University, Dekalb, IL.

12. "Our class enjoyed reading this book and felt that many of the ideas presented were interesting and thought-provoking. The book served as a catalyst for heated class discussion and allowed us an insight into an educational perspective rarely presented." – advanced educational psychology student, University of Richmond, Richmond, VA.

13. "I found *Educating the Entire Person* to be very inspirational. It acknowledged some of my own philosophies as a teacher and allowed me the opportunity to reflect on many other important ideas as well." – student, Elementary Ed. 902, Western Oregon State College.

14. "It has surprised me to know that I've agreed with the majority of what this author has had to say." – student, school of education, Western New Mexico University.

What Should Be the Role of the Teacher of Children?

One of the essays in this book is entitled "What Should Be the Role of the Teacher of Children?" In March of 1995 I sent the essay to Dr. Malcolm Knowles who, as I mentioned previously, is referred to in the ERIC database as "the father of adult learning theory" (EJ 393238). In his letter to me of March 2, 1995, he stated, "I have just finished reading your essay. I am so inspired, I feel like going out and running for Superintendent of Schools! .... The essay is clear, convincing and concise. It is a beauty!"

After sending the essay to Malcolm, and in part because he was so enthusiastic about it, I sent it to the directors/contact persons of 135 homeschooling groups nationwide to determine its relevance to homeschoolers. From that mailing I received twenty-six letters or notes and one phone call from homeschooling groups in eighteen states expressing approval of the essay, and none opposing the essay. Many of those responding praised the essay in glowing terms. In addition, at least four of the homeschooling groups – one a statewide homeschooling association – have published the essay in their newsletters. They are:

1. *Pennsylvania Home Education News* (Issue #19).

2. *Otherways* – Victoria, Australia (Issue #66).

3. *Mentor* – Home Education League of Parents (Aug.& Sept. 1995).

4. *Homefires* (Aug./Sept. 1995).

I believe the overwhelmingly positive responses I received to "What Should Be the Role of the Teacher of Children?" indicates that a majority of homeschooling parents nationwide would come out in support of the views presented in the essay if they all were to read it. Yet, "What Should Be the Role of the Teacher of Children?" proposes a method of education which is opposite to the way children are taught in American schools today. Since, according to one estimate I have heard, as many as one million children in the U.S are now being homeschooled, it is logical to conclude that there exists in the United States today the potential for a national uprising against the current way youngsters are taught in America's schools. I hope *Educating the Entire Person* will contribute to that uprising.

An Imparter of Knowledge

One of the essays in this book is entitled, "An Imparter of Knowledge." Toward the end of 1996, I contacted and then corresponded with the prominent educator, Dr. E. Paul Torrance, a highly respected and internationally known educational psychologist and child educator who, for twelve years, was head of the educational psychology department at the University of Georgia. He was appointed by the President of the United States to be Forum Chairman of the Early Childhood Group of the White House Conference on Children in 1970.

In his letter to me of February 7, 1997, he said,"Thanks for sending me your essay on <u>An Imparter of Knowledge</u>. Your philosophy of teaching is very similar to my own." Dr. Torrance has written the foreword to *Educating the Entire Person*.

Student Unrest

Last year, a publication was sent to me from the Sacramento, California area called *Drop Out*, which is an outlet for kids and adolescents to voice their dissatisfaction with and/or contempt for their schools, as well as offering healthy alternatives for living and learning. This newspaper receives many letters from all over the country from students vehemently opposed to their schools and alienated by them. The newspaper also advertises student publications in which students complain about the schools they attend. From reading the letters and accounts of angry and unhappy young students, and seeing the various other publications students have come up with as a means of venting their dissatisfaction with their schools, it is clear to me that many youngsters hate the policies and practices of the schools they attend, and view their schools as detention and punishment centers rather than as places suitable for learning or living. The current (1997) address of the newspaper is: Drop Out; 1114 21st Street; Sacramento, CA 95814.

Here is a brief sampling of student comments about their schools – just the tip of the iceberg – which were submitted by *Drop Out* readers during the years 1996 and 1997. The eleventh set of comments were sent to me by a fifteen year old high school student who wanted to send a message to individuals considering becoming teachers. I have published that individual's comments in their entirety.

1. "I want teachers to stop their baseless superiority complex over their students."– student, California.

2. "The majority of kids I talk to today say they hate school, and with good reason too."– student, Michigan.

3. "For so many years, I've talked to people who felt damaged by their experiences in school."– student, Indiana.

4. "I realized after my first midterms that school was sucking all the creativity out of me. I was slowly rotting away. I was truly miserable and was very suicidal." – student, Mira Loma High School.

5. "My experiences with parochial education have not only left me with bad memories, but with permanent scars."– student, California.

6. "School robbed me of being in love with life. I was depressed, apathetic, lethargic, tired and oppressed. Now I look and see my friends like this and feel terrible for them."– student who has recently quit school, MA.

7. "I hate school and would like to get a subscription to Drop Out so I can learn how to cope without having to kill or mutilate myself. .... I am sixteen and I go to a public school in Montreal, Canada."

8. "I am 17 and starting my final year of hell in September."– student, somewhere in the U.S.A.

9. "I hated middle school .... I hate high school a lot more."– student, somewhere in the U.S.A.

10. "High school is something to hate. Most of us need something to hate for awhile."– student, MA.

11. "Don't be a teacher unless you are fully aware of, and like what you are getting into. Teaching is something that is done to kids. Most of your students won't want to be in your classes, and won't care about what you talk about when you are talking at (or occasionally with) them. Teaching means taking away play, socialization and sunny afternoons from kids as young as four. Teaching means power to decide when thirty-five other people go to the bathroom, chew, speak, stand, and when and what they study. (To a large extent, what they think.) Teaching means crowd control of 35 children who want to climb trees and play tag and dance and fight and kiss and get muddy. Teaching means being the target of anger and bitterness from young people. Teaching means doing the dirty work for an indoctrination camp. Teaching means blurring the individuality of young people. Teaching means dehumanizing

21

yourself in the eyes of children. Teaching treats kids like cattle in a feedlot, and teachers are only one step up from the cattle. Teaching means taking away the dignity of young people. Teachers are not paid to put their heart into their work. You will not be rewarded if you happen to care. There are many ways to share knowledge with young people, inspire them, make a difference in their lives. Teaching is not one of them. On the contrary, teaching is about becoming an autocratic prison guard. Teaching makes kids miserable and teachers inadvertently support an institution that teaches repression, submission, anger and misanthropy in America's kids. Teaching is immoral. I just wanted you to know that. Please don't be a teacher. Teaching hurts." – student, age 15, Capital High School, Olympia, WA.

A few years ago, a school teacher I was then friends with named Karen sent me a story written by a twelfth grade student who committed suicide the same year. I keep it posted on a bulletin board in my office at home. It inspired me to write the chapter in this book entitled "Can Students Learn Effectively When Their Learning Is Not Mandatory?" The story by the twelfth grade student is typed on one tightly packed sheet of legal paper, and vividly describes a student whose individuality and freedom of expression were crushed by a teacher, parents and school system who conspired to make him do the things in school which were required of him. The story clearly points out that as school requirements closed in on this student's individuality and freedom of expression, and eventually eclipsed them, the student could stand it no longer and took his own life.

In behalf of those people who think I may be exaggerating the harmful effects of traditional methods of educating youngsters, I will quote Charles E. Silberman's introduction to his bestselling book, *Crisis in the Classroom*, which was the result of an expensive three and one half year study of America's public schools commissioned by the Carnegie Corporation of New York. The book earned six national education awards, including the John Dewey award of the National Federation of Teachers. It sold over 100,000 copies in hard-cover and 240,000 copies in paperback. It was selected by the American Library Association as a notable book for 1970 and by The New York Times Book Review as one of the twelve outstanding books for the year. It should be noted that Charles Silberman and his team of researchers visited hundreds of school systems throughout the United States. Here, then, is what Charles Silberman had to say about America's schools for children (*Crisis in the Classroom*, p.10): "It is not possible to spend any prolonged period visiting public school classrooms without being appalled by the mutilation visible everywhere – mutilation of spontaneity, of joy in learning, of pleasure in creating, of sense of self. .... Because adults take the schools so much for granted, they fail to appreciate what grim, joyless places most American schools are, how oppressive and petty are the rules by which they are governed, how intellectually sterile and esthetically barren the atmosphere, what an appalling lack of civility obtains on the part of teachers and principals, what contempt they unconsciously display for children as children." On page 349, he referred to the "repressive, almost prison-like atmosphere of most high schools." Although his book was published by Random House in 1970, change is usually slow to occur on a national scale, which causes me to believe that roughly the same statements could be made about today's schools for youngsters.

Bringing Charles Silberman's negative evaluation of our public schools nearer to the present is John Holt's evaluation of them. In the new preface to his book, *How Children Learn*, published in 1982, three years before his death, John Holt said,"Since I wrote this book our schools (for children) have, with few exceptions, moved steadily and often rapidly in the wrong direction. Schools are on the whole bigger than they used to be, more depersonalized, more threatening, more dangerous. What they try to teach is even more fragmented than it was, i.e., not connected with anything else, and hence meaningless. Teachers have even less to say than they used to about what they teach and how they teach and test it. The schools cling more and more stubbornly to their mistaken idea that education and teaching are industrial processes, to be designed and planned from above in the minutest detail and then imposed on passive teachers and their even more passive students."

I hope all people, and especially college students studying to be teachers, take a close look at what America's children and adolescents think of the schools they attend. If schools for youth in America are ever to adequately serve the needs of the students, extensive research that is not biased in favor of teachers and administrators needs to be done to uncover the truth about what America's youth think of their schools, and the results must be widely published. If this research is honestly and comprehensively undertaken, I believe it will be found that far too often the primary goals of America's schools (for youngsters) are:

1. To manage rather than help students.

2. To further the goals of educational administrators rather than the legitimate needs of the students.

3. To perpetuate a failing system to retain tax dollars and other funding.

I believe it is also important to reassess the aims of higher education. Institutions of higher education pride themselves in how efficiently they can impart knowledge, but usually do not sufficiently consider how their students are reacting to the process of being taught. Personalizing and individualizing the learning process for the sake of the comfort, satisfaction, fulfillment and growth patterns of college students is usually not a priority of educators of adults; and, as a result, college students often suffer needlessly, while their creativity, initiative and individuality are stifled and undermined. Adapting subject matter and methods of instruction to the learning needs and response patterns of individual students would result in a very different type of education than can be obtained by pressuring students to adapt to a preestablished curricula and preestablished methods of instruction. One could argue that this method of education would result in poorer skill acquisition and job preparation; but it can also be argued that a more emotionally and mentally integrated human being is a more productive worker and a better citizen.

My Background and Qualifications

Many of the college students who critiqued *Educating the Entire Person* wanted to know something about me, in particular my background and qualifications for writing *Educating the Entire Person*. Judged by the normal criteria used for determining credibility for authoring a book of ideas about the educational process, I would be deemed a terrible disappointment because I do not have a college degree in psychology or education, nor have I taught school or raised children. My path into the subject of educational theory was untraditional, but it was legitimate.

As a young man, I worked briefly as a noon aide at a public elementary school, and witnessed the harmful effects caused by

24

thc school's policy of controlling many aspects of the children's behavior in lunch lines, during lunch and recess and when children were in transit between classes. Some of my duties were: noise control (the children became quite noisy while eating their lunches and I was supposed to suppress the level of their noise); making sure the children behaved in an orderly manner (for example, making sure they formed and stayed in a uniform line while waiting at the cafeteria for their lunches); making sure the children were at their appointed locations during recess; making sure the children did not run except while playing sports; quelling disruptive behavior and curtailing unconventional behavior. The kids resented the controls that were placed on them, and some of them rebelled. Other children were stifled by the controls and they repressed behavior which many people would consider healthy and normal. My job description was identical with what might be the job description of a sheep dog: making sure the flock does what the master wants it to do, and does not stray. I believe the underlying reasons for the controls placed upon the kids by school authorities were: to make sure the children behaved as much like adults as possible, so that the school would have as few discipline problems as possible and would maintain a good image in the mind of the public and local educational authorities.

Growing up, I tried to conform to the learning and attendance requirements of the U.S. Education system because I loved ideas and wanted to learn; but try as I might, I could not perform well within the system. By age sixteen, I was a serious writer, and tried to analyze and understand my problem by writing about it. I believed my motives for wanting to learn were praiseworthy, that my thinking ability was more than adequate, and that I possessed a willingness to apply myself. So what was wrong? I eventually concluded the primary fault was with the education system itself rather than with me.

It has taken me many years to unravel the riddle of what is wrong with U.S. educational methods. I had to plumb the depths of my subconscious mind over a period of many years, all the while seeking counsel from my own analytical abilities, and only gradually got glimpses of the truth.

The bulk of *Educating the Entire Person* did not result from reading and mulling over other people's theories of education. The 1994 edition, (pp. 11-12 & pp. 27-135), was written prior to my having any knowledge of educational theory or the

25

history of education other than having read *Summerhill* by A.S. Neill more than thirty years ago. Since writing the 1994 edition of *Educating the Entire Person*, I have been slowly trying to acquire a basic knowledge of educational theory and the history of education.

– Ron Dultz   August, 1997

THERE ARE FIVE ULTIMATE OBJECTIVES WHEN EDUCATING OUR YOUNGSTERS

If a youngster's education is to be effective, and of enduring value, I believe that five ultimate objectives need to be accomplished. One of the five objectives is to make sure his or her education satisfies the requirement each individual has to develop naturally, in accordance with the youngster's abilities, inclinations, needs and growth patterns. Another of the objectives is that of equipping the youngster with the skills to be self-sufficient financially and with the skills to be able to manage his own affairs by the time his circumstances determine, or his society mandates, that he must move out into the world as an autonomous being and begin fending for himself. A third objective is that of moral development. A fourth objective is that of assisting the youngster in her efforts to develop a clear, precise and satisfactory identity of her own. And the fifth objective, which is the one that has long been favored in our schools, is that of enriching the student from a cultural standpoint and offering him or her a broad range of factual knowledge.

Of these five educational objectives, four are critical. The only one which can be left unaccomplished without serious detriment to a youngster is the one which has been favored by our country's system of education: that of cultural enrichment and the acquiring of a broad range of factual knowledge. While cultural enrichment and the acquiring of a broad range of factual knowledge have definite value, they are not as important as the other four educational objectives.

If our people are going to be healthy, happy and capable, our educational system from preschool onward must fully address the problems of human development and the requirements of adulthood concurrent with attempting to transmit information and knowledge of various kinds. In our modern times, life is abrupt, and the safety and security of parental care does not last long after eighteen years of age; and our society, itself, has very little commitment to coddling us and protecting us after we have reached eighteen years of age. So our preparedness for life and our sense of our self must be given a superb foundation while we are still growing up if we are going to survive in this world, and be a fit match for its demands and challenges. And, for most youngsters, there are only two places in which these things can be accomplished: in the home and in school; but parents are not professional educators, and may not have the ability, the tools or the time to influence the development of their children in all the ways that are needed. It is, therefore, a proper and befitting job of our teachers and schools to take on these challenges; and, in fact, it is essential that they do so if our society is going to be a strong one which strives to fulfill the needs of its people.

No effort should be spared in ensuring that our young people will be *fully equipped* for supporting themselves financially and managing their own affairs by the time they have reached eighteen years of age, or by the time they are expected to fend for themselves and make their own way in the world. And no effort should be spared in ensuring that the quality of their morals is evolving nicely at the same time. And no effort should be spared in ensuring that the whole of their education coincides with their own needs, inclinations and growth patterns. And no effort should be spared in helping each youngster move forward in a sensitive and complex search for himself. To do less is to do our young people a great disservice; and will, indeed, endanger both them and our society. Since public and private schools are often better equipped for these tasks than parents, and already occupy a large percentage of each youngster's time, it is important that they (the schools) commit themselves fully to the proper development of the youngsters they instruct, and that they do so in a comprehensive manner.

Educating our youngsters in a manner that is in compliance with all five previously mentioned educational objectives, and paying the closest attention to the four objectives that are the most critical, would be a comprehensive and effective approach to education. However, since our current system of educating our young people is so heavily weighted in favor of cultural enrichment and the acquiring of a broad range of factual knowledge, and seriously neglects the other four educational objectives; the curriculum used for educating our youngsters, and the teaching methods and teaching tools employed, must be critically examined; and, where necessary, reformed or replaced. This is easier said than done because the old ways of doing things and looking at them within the system of education that is predominant in this country are reinforced by years of tradition and habit.

Sometimes the only way of taking an honest look at something is by eliminating the customary way of perceiving it; and, sometimes, the only way of honestly evaluating a procedure or practice is by having no prejudice in its favor. I find this rule to be most beneficial in coming to terms with many things; and, I have found it essential in trying to penetrate into the heart of what formal education should, and can, do for our young people. So that I can have an opportunity to elaborate effectively on my concept of the five educational objectives, I will ask you, the reader, to temporarily forget all you have been taught about the role of the teacher and the role of the student. And I would like you to temporarily forget all you have been taught about the role of our schools and the nature of the educational process that occurs within them. If you will first do that for me, I then would like you to join me on an adventure in which we will explore a different way of looking at the educational process, and a fresh approach to educating our youngsters.

Let us start anew with the very first young pupils in the very first school. There are now no existing references for educating our children or young people. You and I are asked to design and implement a system for educating a small group of youngsters in their own best interest. We want to prepare the students for what life will require of them as adults, and for what they will require of themselves. We want them to end up being adults who are self-sufficient, happy and capable, who have integrity and good character, and who will contribute to the well-being of society; or, at least, not detract from its well-being. Let us assume we are given the right to influence these youngsters, who are from five to eighteen years of age, six hours per day, five days per week, and let us assume that we are provided with salaries for ourselves, school grounds, a school-house, and money for teaching equipment, books and other tools of the trade. And we are given full and complete responsibility for the education of these youngsters. How will we proceed, and what will our educational objectives be? Well, I'm not sure how you will proceed, and what your educational objectives will be, but I'm fairly certain how I will proceed, and what my educational objectives will be.

My educational objectives will be far easier to decide than my procedures for implementing those objectives because implementing them would depend upon the particular requirements of each student I am instructing, and upon his or her responses to the items, methods and tools of instruction I am using for that purpose. I realize that the educational items, methods and tools I employ, regardless of their merit, are useless unless they can be adapted to the needs, inclinations and growth patterns of my students. Each young student is a human being who exists in a certain form. He has certain thoughts, emotions, needs, and certain capacities, abilities and inclinations. If I am to be successful in instructing, I must do so in a way that is suitable to each individual youngster; and the more successfully I can relate to each youngster's individual learning needs, the better educator I can be. I realize that I cannot hope to instruct any youngster effectively unless I become the servant of his most urgent and pressing educational needs. I realize that I will fail badly in teaching anything if I do not pay close attention to each youngster's individual learning needs and requirements, and work within that framework; regardless of how well equipped I am as a teacher, and regardless of how good my school grounds, schoolhouse, teaching equipment and teaching tools are.

Now that I have established the framework in which I shall teach, I am ready to concern myself with the substance of what I shall teach the youngsters. Rather than begin with specifics, I wish to establish general educational objectives that I feel are most appropriate and beneficial for the youngsters; and, afterward, I will figure out the specific items of instruction, and the methods and tools I will employ to try to convey those to my young students.

As an instructor of the total person, I consider the society in which I live in order to determine what will be required of my young students upon completion of their studies because I want to formulate my teaching objectives with that in mind. I determine that the youngsters I am to instruct will be growing up in a society which demands that each youngster be able to manage his own affairs and provide for his own financial needs by the age of eighteen; that is, if his parents or guardians are unwilling, or unable, to continue to do so. This is a glaring fact, one I cannot ignore if I am to be a responsible caretaker of the overall development and educational needs of the youngsters I am to instruct. And so, one of the central objectives of my instruction will be to provide each student with strong money-making skills and a thorough preparation for managing his own affairs and fending for himself in all the ways that will be required of him once he has reached eighteen years of age, or once he is required to go out on his own in the world. I realize that if a major portion of the educational process from age five through age eighteen is devoted to this, each student will have learned a lot about getting along on his/her own in the world by the end of that time, and should also have acquired some legitimate money-making skills. Hopefully, this will enable a student of mine to enter the world at age eighteen equipped and confident if it becomes necessary or desirable to do so, instead of being a mere burden to himself, his parents and society. Instead of feeling helpless and worthless, like many young adults do, he will have dignity and pride, and the foundation for making a good life for himself. She will be able to start life as a capable person, making a real direction for herself, instead of as an incompetent one, at the mercy of everyone and everything within her society.

As an instructor of the total person, I realize that it is essential for each of my students to develop a satisfactory and well-defined identity of his/her own. I also realize that a student may acquire a great deal of facts, information and skills; yet if he does not have a satisfactory and well-defined identity of his own, he will not be an effective person, or a happy one. I understand that developing a well-defined and satisfactory identity of one's own is a complicated, sensitive and personal process, but one in which a teacher who is knowledgeable about life may play a part. Consequently, I will make a special effort to contribute to this aspect of each of my student's education, and I will make sure that I am never responsible for distracting my students from accomplishing this most important mission.

As an instructor of the total person, I delve into everything that I am, and have learned about life, to determine what great morals and values I must impart to my young students; and I decide that all of them can be summed up in one word: character. I realize that information, knowledge and skills serve no purpose if they are not embraced by someone whose character is strong and good. Consequently, the inculcation of good character must be an essential part of my teaching if it is ultimately going to go for a good purpose. From the very beginning, then, I will spare no effort in helping my young students grow into people who are strong, good, kind and wise. I will take special pains in pointing out to them that all knowledge is to be used for the ultimate purposes of: living a fulfilling and constructive life; being good to people and making their lives better; and advancing all the things that are honorable, good and beautiful in life.

Lastly, I will try to imbue my students with a broad range of factual knowledge and with the cultural refinements of life, so that they will have as much as possible to select from in fashioning their lives; and in living them in an enlightened, sensitive, thoughtful and artistic manner.

These, then, are the five teaching objectives I will assign myself as one of the very first teachers in the very first school; which, as you can see, are the original educational objectives I presented at the beginning of this essay. The rest of the details of instructing the youngsters I am to teach, as to methods and items of instruction, and the type of instructional tools and equipment to be used, are of less importance; and I can attend to them in good time.

We can now return from this foray into an imaginary setting, for I have made the points I intended. I wish to thank the reader's indulgence, and ask that we now move on to additional aspects of my theory of educating the entire person.

THE THREE PHASES OF GROWING UP

Just as we can more easily understand the workings of an automobile if we separate it into its major components, such as engine, transmission, electrical system, cooling system, and so forth; we can more easily understand the process of growing up if we separate it into its major components.

I view the process of growing up as occurring in three distinct phases. The first phase I call the *orientation* phase. This is the phase young children go through in which they react to things uninhibitedly, spontaneously and often clumsily. Their identity as individuals is very uncertain and poorly developed. They know little about who they are and about what they should be doing. They are unskilled in planning, thinking things through, and organizing their time. They depend upon others to provide them with the main part of their emotional and psychological support, and know little about fending for themselves or looking after their own needs. They are children in the truest and most complete sense of the term. In actuality, they are orienting themselves to the things to be found in their immediate environment, to the various things outside of their immediate environment that come to their attention; and even to their own needs, feelings, thoughts, inclinations, habits and response patterns.

I refer to the second phase of growing up as the *experience seeking* phase. This applies to the time in which youngsters are demonstrating ability to think things through; and already have a burgeoning and somewhat confident sense of themselves as specific individuals with specific needs, interests, habits, feelings, inclinations and thoughts. They have outgrown the extremely vulnerable and confused phase of childhood, and are ready for hearty participation beyond the safe environment of the home. This readiness is genuine if they can take control of themselves as independent beings beyond the safe environment of the home within limitations adapted to their age and capabilities. The exact age at which this readiness occurs will vary with each youngster, and will depend somewhat on his or her circumstances. In a small town, or rural environment, a youngster who can independently get to a nearby market a few blocks away, and return safely with a few groceries for mom, has entered the second phase of growing up. This is a time for seeking experiences of every kind which can facilitate the process of learning and understanding. The more worthwhile and wide-ranging the life experiences of a youngster are during this phase of growing up, and the better he or she can relate to them and benefit from them, the faster the youngster will grow up and mature. It is the quality of a youngster's experiences, and the quality of his ability to relate to and benefit from those experiences, that determine if his youth is well spent or not.

The third phase of a youngster's path of growing up, I refer to as the *deciding* phase. This is usually the late teens, and beyond. It is a time in which a young person, making use of years of testing and trying different things, experiencing many different things, and being exposed to many different philosophies and points of view, begins to firmly decide who she really is, what she wants to do with her life, and what she wants to ultimately become: in terms of her professional life, personal characteristics and way of life. These ultimate objectives, of course, are not written in stone because they will most likely be altered or changed with the passage of time; but they can nonetheless be formulated, and referred to as a direction-finding tool.

While these three phases of growing up are distinctive, they often overlap; and aspects of one phase may often be found occurring within one of the other phases. When this is the case, it can be said that a youngster is *predominantly* in phase one, two or three of growing up.

Having expressed these opening paragraphs to clarify my concept of the three phases of growing up, I would like now to share with the reader some further thoughts that have occurred to me on each of these three phases. I'd like to begin again with the first phase of growing up, which I have labeled the *orientation* phase, and then elaborate more fully on phases two and three of growing up, in that order.

It is naturally important that youngsters in the initial phase of growing up, which I have termed the *orientation* phase, be viewed by adults and others through the appropriate pair of glasses. For, how we perceive them will result in how we will relate to them; and, consequently, in the effect we shall have upon their lives. If we view children as unruly little beings who must be contained and controlled, we are not viewing them in a a responsible manner. If we view children as little more than nuisances who must be provided for, we will be poor caretakers of their future; and we will be interfering with, and actually blocking, the magical and delicate process of their growing up and becoming people of true merit and value.

It is incumbent upon all adults, and others, to treat children with respect; and to grant that childhood has a dignity of its own. Though children are unruly, may often be a nuisance or troublesome, and may often get into mischief and create endless little problems and difficulties for their caretakers and providers; it is important that they not be made to feel inferior, and are not persecuted, on this account. They cannot help being children any more than we can help being adults. Even though it is difficult, or impossible, for the adult mind to view the little acts of mischief of children, or their unruly or chaotic behavior, as being worthwhile; and even though it is difficult, or impossible, for the adult mind to find real substance or meaning in the often trivial activities, pursuits and preoccupations of children, we can lend a dignity to those activities, pursuits and preoccupations by understanding that the dynamics behind them are truly magical and important. And that is because those dynamics, and the activities they produce, are an essential part of the overall process of growing up and becoming a complete person.

Viewed as part of a dynamic process that can have a very poignant, beautiful and meaningful outcome, the activities of children, no matter how trivial, troublesome or nonsensical they may appear, become awe-inspiring and worthy of our most profound appreciation. We must respect children's natural tendencies and inclinations if they are native to childhood; and, those of their actions and activities we do not understand, we must give the benefit of the doubt and allow to exist, unless those actions or activities endanger life and limb. We must never try to suppress the natural functions and processes that are fundamental parts of their childhood natures. To do so is to stifle and frustrate children when they most need our support and encouragement. We must plainly give children a vote of confidence based upon the things they are and do as children, not based upon what we think they should do, nor upon how adults are expected to behave. While we can encourage children to improve and grow up; we must love, cherish and respect them *as they are*, and not pressure them to grow up and mature before they are ready.

Because growing up is a difficult process for most of us; and because growing up is a fragile and delicate process, susceptible to obstacles and impediments of all kinds; it is important for children to be confident in their ability to grow up into competent and capable human beings. Therefore, they must believe that their childish natures, and their activities as children, have worth; and they must be allowed to pour themselves into their childish natures, and fully experience the uniqueness, power and intensity of them. Strong, assertive and energetic adults are the outgrowth of strong, assertive and energetic children. So, it seems that an important gauge of the success of a youngster's childhood years is the intensity and purpose with which they are lived; and this fact may be of greater importance to the child's well-being and future development than his or her accomplishments in performing tasks or demonstrating abilities which are adult in nature. Thus, a restless or rebellious child, or a child prone to ingenious shenanigans and acts of mischief, might be seen, by virtue of these characteristics, to be exhibiting wonderful potential for strength of identity and character. This is so because we are evaluating his actions according to the needs and capacities of children; and not according to the standards of excellence that are applied to the behavior of adults.

If it is true that an important gauge of the success of a youngster's childhood years is the intensity and purpose with which they are lived; and if it is true that strong, assertive and energetic adults are usually the outgrowth of strong, assertive and energetic children; a teacher's first responsibility to each child, whose development and instruction she is responsible for, is to preserve and encourage the intensity, enthusiasm and individuality of the child's native instincts and inclinations, regardless of the form in which they appear. When they are seen as an integral part of childhood, wild behavior, disorderly behavior, untamed curiosity, rebellion, and odd or unusual behavior can be endorsed by the teacher who wishes the best for her young students.

In conjunction with endorsing the instincts and inclinations native to childhood, the teacher can try her best to influence the child's native instincts and inclinations toward more sophisticated avenues of expression, such as toward skilled articulation of thoughts and feelings. The same intensity of emotion that is expressed in a wild scream, for example, can be expressed in a well-thought-out statement. To preserve the intensity and enthusiasm of a child's native instincts and inclinations, as opposed to threatening them, a teacher must first of all condone them. The child should not be made to feel ashamed of, nor should he be chastised for, intense or enthusiastic behavior of his own invention. For, it is not for us to place a value on the child's behavior; rather, it is our responsibility to preserve and encourage the individuality, intensity and enthusiasm that is behind it. If we criticize or try to control the child's behavior, we are doing the same to the beautiful and natural emotions that support it. Though a teacher feels she knows how to improve a child's mind or life, she must not usurp the psychological and emotional needs of the child by imposing her will upon the child. Any instruction that is not willingly received or sought by a youngster has potentially damaging results. Ideally, the teacher should not pressure the child, and should impose on him as few rules as possible. The child should feel that wherever he gets to in his learning is a result of his own momentum. That is, he should be inspired to get there − not pushed, forced, prodded or pulled. As long as you are working with and not against the child's individuality, instincts, needs and inclinations, you are providing wind to his sails. The other way, you are providing the sails and expecting him to be the wind. You are simply trying to make the child into an image of yourself.

In my opinion, the teacher should actually encourage kids to find their own voices and ways of doing things as a coach might cheer on his athletes. The more intense, enthusiastic and individualistic the children are, the greater should be the teacher's joy. Once the teacher has helped to preserve and encourage the native instincts, natural inclinations, individualistic tendencies, untamed energy and power of her young students, she has something inspiring to work with. Then she has the fire, and need only apply the logs. Once she has helped to preserve and encourage the blaze that is prepared to burn up all obstacles, she may, with full confidence, tempt it with more sophisticated and articulate outlets; but outlets that do not diminish the power and energy of that blaze by a fraction.

Once the teacher sees that vitality, individuality, strength and power are not lacking in her young students; that, indeed each of them has experienced in him or her self a true lust and joy for life, a true freedom of expression and force of personality, the teacher can envision her young students progressing great lengths and toward great ends. She can rest assured knowing that her young students know what power, pride, enthusiasm and the intense pursuit of their own individuality are, as they have already experienced them. They have found them in themselves, in the selves they understand, which are none other than their childish, unorganized, chaotic and undisciplined selves. Now these same qualities need only be applied within a more sophisticated framework. It does not really matter how long it takes before a teacher's presentation of more sophisticated things catches on; that is, before the child turns his or her individuality, energy and power in their direction. The thing of main importance is that the blaze, the momentum, the energy, the individuality, the integrity and the power native to childhood be preserved; and, somehow, encouraged.

Naturally, a group of youngsters so instructed would appear to some, or to many, to belong in reform school. Some people will say they are being allowed to be animals, that civilization is being defied. But truly enlightened people will take great pride in the children's vigor and freedom of expression. They will judge their activities by their context: that of childhood; and so, will not condemn them for lacking adult refinement.

In advocating freedom of expression for children, I am not advocating anarchy, nor am I in opposition to the idea of providing the lives of children with some structure as an aid in helping them to feel secure; or so that they will have a framework in which to conduct their activities, when that is needed. I am simply asserting that children have the right to live fully their lives as children and to do all the things that are natural for children to do. A child's life should be lived as he needs to live it, in such a way as pleases him. It should not be lived according to the way an adult decides it must be lived. And the learning that children do should be of their own choosing; and in harmony with their own needs, desires and growth patterns. Naturally, children should be taught to respect the rights and property of others in connection with all their own activities; but because they cannot yet be expected to be fully responsible for their own behavior, I believe that many of their transgressions should be tolerated or forgiven.

In advocating freedom of expression for children, I do not mean to ignore other aspects of children's education. From the first, children should be helped to learn the basics of speaking, reading, writing and math so that they will have use of these essential tools. As soon as it becomes possible, the teacher should begin teaching children a love for knowledge. Without a love for knowledge, they may have difficulty motivating themselves to learn.

Teaching children a love for knowledge does not mean

teaching kids to become or do anything other than to love knowledge. If a teacher can succeed at teaching kids to love knowledge, she will have done them one of the greatest services possible toward the end of making them good students. A good student is not one who learns because he or she is pressured or forced to do so. A good student is first and foremost one who has a great and enduring love for knowledge, and pursues learning with the intensity and relentlessness of that love. And how does a teacher teach students to love knowledge? Well, firstly, the teacher must have a very sincere and very great love for knowledge. If she does not, she is really wasting her time trying to teach it to her students, as they will see through her. Teaching someone to love knowledge is purely and simply an endeavor in esthetics: "Come, my students, and partake with me of some of the wonders of knowledge. I shall be your guide through a most astounding history of the achievements of humankind, the miracles of nature and the prospects for the future. Leave your skepticism behind, for this is a time to rejoice. Do not think I am here to bore you or thrust any task upon you. I offer but a tour of joy, and all those open to see that which is worthy of appreciation need but look with me as I guide us along some of the more beautiful and clearly cut paths of knowledge." Such would be the teacher's approach and method. She would have no hidden motive. Indeed, it would not be any more of a drudgery than walking through a museum of knowledge built for children or watching a fascinating documentary suitable for children. If students are not initially responsive to such a wide presentation, a teacher may elect to work with students individually to expand their appreciation of knowledge along the lines of their interests or inclinations. After the teacher, with this method, has imbued in her students a love of knowledge, it will be much easier for her to influence them to become precise and effective human beings.

In teaching children a love for knowledge, in helping them to learn the basics of speaking, reading, writing and math, or in instructing them at anything whatsoever, the teacher must always remember that, no matter how urgently she wants the child to become a precise and effective human being, learning is the student's adventure. The student must be given the responsibility for his or her education right from the beginning. Right from the beginning, the teacher must instruct the student that, as a teacher, her role is limited and necessarily handicapped; that her job is to assist the student in his or her learning and development; that if the student is not making an effort to become involved in learning those skills and subjects which are of interest to him, the teacher cannot properly assist him.

In addition to trying to teach children a love of knowledge, trying to impart to them the basics of speaking, reading, writing and math, and trying to reinforce the habits, tendencies, needs and inclinations that are native to childhood, a teacher must teach children with some ultimate objectives in mind. In the first section of this book, I listed the ones I consider essential to each young student's education. One of those which I listed, if you will recall, is the student's need to be self-sufficient and manage his own affairs by the time he reaches eighteen years of age; or by the time he or she is expected to move out into the world as an autonomous being. If growing up is to culminate in the ability to be self-sufficient and manage one's own affairs, it is logical and correct to conclude that the years of growing up, and the learning process itself, must be heavily weighted with those activities which challenge youngsters' decision-making capacities and tendencies toward self-sufficiency. This means that children, young students and emerging young adults should not be overly protected; but should be given every opportunity for trial and error, success and failure, in their various activities and choices; and should be expected to be responsible for themselves, and for their activities as students, in ever-increasing degrees. Adults should not intervene to do things for youngsters or emerging young adults, nor make decisions for them, in matters they are capable of attempting on their own, even though their failure may be inevitable. Failure is but the first step toward success; and, if we are not permitted to fail, we can never hope to succeed. The decision-making process, and efforts at self-reliance and self-sufficiency, are relevant aspects of everything a youngster undertakes, including his formal education.

If the decision-making process is denied to children, or is undermined or diluted by instructors or school administrators who think they know what is best concerning what and how children should study, children are being violated in two important ways. First, their freedom of choice is being taken away from them. They are being told that they do not have a right to do what they genuinely feel like doing and are inclined to do, even though doing it would hurt no one. This is wrong.

Second, they are being deprived of the right to think things through and decide things for themselves. This prevents them from growing up. The solution is to restore to all children *the right to select their own subject matter to be learned, and the right to design their own learning procedure* – with assistance provided by the teacher, if it is needed or sought. (I'll elaborate on this proposition in subsequent sections of this treatise.)

It is appalling to consider that children at home, young students, and emerging young adults are treated similarly in that they are so often coddled, protected, provided for and decided for until they are finally expected to be on their own, think for themselves, make their own decisions and be self-sufficient. Because this is the case, it is not surprising that so many of our young people grow up being mixed up and confused in the handling of their own affairs, are ill-equipped to fend for themselves in the world; and wind up being a burden upon society instead of a credit to it.

This brings me once again to the second phase of a person's development – the *experience seeking* phase. After the child has really learned to express himself in terms of being a child, and has fully participated in childhood for whatever amount of time it is suitable for him to do so, he will be ready to focus his energies on seeking experiences. In the *orientation* phase, a child also seeks experiences; but does so more for the purpose of adjusting to one's immediate surroundings than for reaching out beyond them. One might say that as a youngster grows up, he or she becomes less focused on adjusting to one's immediate surroundings and more focused on experiencing what lies beyond them.

This second phase of a person's development consists of exposing oneself to things on a large scale in order to give oneself a broad range of experience. The purpose of this is for the person to obtain enough experience to eventually be able to make mature decisions concerning what one's goals will be, how one is going to live one's life, and what values and principles one will adopt as one's own. There are many experiences that cannot be considered worthwhile for this because they do not have anything to do with the essentials of life. Many experiences that do not, at first glance, seem relevant to the essentials of life may prove to be quite pertinent upon closer examination. Raising goldfish, for example, may seem to have little to do with the essentials of life. But if a young person learns from this a sense of responsibility, and learns to be more gentle and caring, its contributions to his overall value as a human being become obvious.

Obtaining experience is an art in itself. A person who is at the second phase of his development, that is, the *experience seeking* phase, needs a realization of how to efficiently go about obtaining experience. There seems to be a way of doing everything. There's a way to drive a car, a way to pilot a plane, a way to play football. What is the way of obtaining experience? It seems to me that the only way to be sure of obtaining a wide range of experience is to become an obtainer of experience; that is, obtaining experience must become one's chief activity. Obtaining experience as a regular and consistent activity requires a certain frame of mind. One must be adventurous and intensely curious. The basis for these attributes, if they are to be effective, must be good solid reasons, such as wanting to know about people, about life and about oneself. With strong contact with such reasons in the foreground of one's thoughts, and a willingness to act upon them, one simply cannot avoid a fruitful experience-seeking effort.

One who is attempting to gather experience should always look for and then pursue all the things and nuances of life with which he feels any association until his association with each is resolved in his mind, or until his association with each has been dissolved or fulfilled. All of us run across incidents that move us, persons who intrigue or excite us, things that for one reason or another appeal to us; yet, how seldom it is that we catch ourselves at one of those moments and say to ourselves: "There's something going on here that has meaning to me out of the ordinary. It would seem to be wise to pursue it; for I may find out something new about myself, about people, about life; or I might find something for myself." Most of us are just not so attuned to the possibilities within things. This is because we are not in the first place on the lookout for dramatic involvement, for adventure, and for alternative forms of feeling, thinking and being. Perhaps we have a "nothing new under the sun" attitude. Perhaps we feel there is not much to be gained from new experiences.

I feel that if a person is not prepared to become involved, even to go on a long adventure, at the slightest nuance in life that he senses might be meant for him, he will never discover many truths and other things he was meant to discover. And if the young do not pursue anything and everything that intrigues or interests them, they will never approach an understanding of life's vastness, and they will never have a true feeling for its essence and limitations. Life is filled with potentials, accomplishments, abilities, things of use and things of esthetic value; but, to find these things, one must be on the lookout for them, and go look for them and investigate wherever they are thought to be. It is as though we are looking for the ends of their strings. Once we find the end of a string, we need only follow the string back to its beginning; and, along the way, we will find little pots of gold. Once in a while, a person is lucky and stumbles across the end of a long string when he isn't even looking for it; and, presto! his life is renewed. But we should not be so dependent upon the chances of fate. Sometimes weeks or months pass by without a person coming in contact with something toward which he is personally moved. But when something of note finally occurs, when he gets a lead, then is the time for him to compensate for the drought with a vengeance, becoming active to the hilt. He should not miss this chance.

In the second phase of a person's development, the teacher should instruct the student to seek experiences. She should teach him that life is a great and wonderful adventure and that he, the student, is but a ship not yet embarked on the great sea of existence; that beauty, knowledge, grace and power lie awaiting him, but off in the farthest distances, far beyond the range of his present sight; that he must learn to see with the eyes of the world if he is to truly see. The teacher should inspire him to move on to new things frequently, and not to stagnate. She must teach the student that he must become a ship tossed about on the waves of life until he has developed a feel for those waves, as well as a knowledge of their movements, size, color and substance.

This brings me once again to the third phase of growing up, which I have termed the *deciding* phase. The third phase of a person's development consists of defining the contents of life; then determining what one's goals and aims will be, what one's lifestyle or way of life will be, and what one's principles and values will be. Naturally, some aspects of these things have been decided already, or may be in the process of being decided; but there comes a time, and it's called adulthood, when each person must make an all-out effort to make conclusive decisions on all those things which will be pertinent to living a meaningful and successful life. At this third phase of his development, a person must take on a sober aspect, as it is a time of severe concentration. He must decide what it is he will cement into his being; then live for, fight for and even die for. Every young person must sooner or later decide this. Upon making these ultimate decisions, he is an adult, for better or worse. If he fails to make decisions of this severity, if he never steps into the arena of consequence, if he never puts himself at the mercy of his opinions; his own conscience will consume him and he will die – perhaps not a physical death, but a spiritual one. He can put off making the great decisions for a long while, and may well be right to do so; but eventually he must take a stand. If he takes a stand and fails, he can still try again, having learned from his errors. But if he refuses to stand hard and fast with his whole being, if he cannot ever manage the will power and confidence to do it, he is doomed. In deciding in no uncertain terms what his convictions are and what he will do with his life, the student works internally and externally. He works on integrating and understanding the various factors and facets that are himself, and on evaluating philosophies, points of view, facts, circumstances and situations. Whereas before he would go to things mainly for experience, now he must begin to perfect his understanding of them and relationship to them. He must strive to give each and every thing he considers important its meaning, its designated place in the scheme of things, and he must decide what his relationship to each will be. But how will he, the young person, not so long ago a child, arise and walk in the glory of adulthood: a fully comprehending and purposeful being? What miracles could possibly transpose him? Is this not expecting too much? How does a young seedling turn into a giant oak? How does a blind person learn to see like an eagle and a slow one learn to race like an antelope? How can this fledgling become a dynamo of power, thoroughly synchronized and well-directed? He faints at the strange and overwhelming exertions, the contortions of mind, the bizarre encounters that must precede such feats.

Time passes slowly and nervously for the student locked in decision-making of this severity. As it passes, the young student will become a victim of the pain of being suspended between nowhere and somewhere, with no solution in sight. This pain is likely to increase over time as he discovers that his efforts so often seem to be unproductive. Then, one day, after

44

much time has elapsed, much energy has been expended and many struggles have been endured, some strange force seems to lift the student up and propel him forward toward his destiny. That force is himself; but it is some deeply hidden, unconscious part of him. It had been slowly gathering strength. The complexity of his motives elude him. He does not understand what is empowering him or where he is headed. He is one, two, ten steps ahead of himself; and learns to understand many of his decisions years later in retrospect. Had he the faintest idea of how far he would have to travel, he would never have begun the journey.

When he completes his great leaps forward, and sees all the ground he has traversed, he is awed, struck dumb. He seems suddenly to have gained a far advanced understanding and capacity. It is as if he has been suddenly transported far ahead in time. A deep, deep silence invades him: the stillness of eternity. In looking at his newly acquired past, he feels he is looking at himself for the first time. He cannot fathom the depths of his own being. He is a great human being, a hero. He is not a hero in other people's eyes – he is a hero in his own eyes as he has mastered himself in terms of life! And now it is time for mature action. Our young person has become an adult, with a specific set of values and priorities, and a plan for his future.

In the third phase of a person's development, the teacher encourages the student to define the contents of life and decide what he will do with his life. In this connection, the teacher encourages the student to move toward increasingly bold commitments, and to be his own person in every way.

Likely, the goal toward which our new adult has decided to apply the bulk of his energies will require further preparation. Let us assume he wants to become a doctor. He is not a child who wants to become a doctor; he is an adult who wants to become a doctor. This is a very great difference! If he has learned his lessons well, he will proceed as follows. .... He will think long and hard about his decision. Having come to the conclusion that he wants to be a doctor after much uncertainty, involving many months, or years, spent in gut-wrenching and emotional decision-making, he is certainly not going to let the matter just drop as though there were nothing more to it. Such questions will arise as: "Do I want to open up a practice of my own; or concentrate on bringing a knowledge of medicine to the level of the common man, so that each person will be better able to diagnose himself and prevent medical problems from developing, or what? If I want to work as a practicing physician, for whom do I wish to make my services available? Shall I be a pediatrician, or some other type of doctor? Until he has decided such questions, he will proceed cautiously; for this person is no fool. He knows that it is important for one to know, rather than to guess. He knows that the smallest decision, or lack of it, frequently has great consequences. He has learned this the hard way; and so, will definitely prepare himself.

As he knows the folly of blind obedience, our new adult will go to people of learning in the field when he, himself, has some learning in it, so that he will not be swallowed up by them. Ideally, he senses that to work with him with any degree of enthusiasm or intensity, his teachers will have to take an interest in him; that it is therefore important that he be able to challenge them and interest them in their field to some degree before he confronts them as a student.

Since he is an adult, his teachers are going to have to prove themselves to him to some degree before he accepts them as teachers. With him, the teacher will not be able to get by with credentials alone. The teacher will have to have impact as a person, as a thinker and as a doctor.

This young adult will soon be ready to enter into a new drama: that of professional student. It will be his drama, and he should guard it jealously. He will guard it by putting himself at the wheel and allowing no other hands to touch it, not even for an instant. He does not know all that is in store for him, but he will be armed with fine instincts and approach as a result of his knowledge of life, and of himself. Soon he will start to expose himself to literature in his field, to judge for himself what is the wheat and what the chaff. This may not be smooth rolling. For a considerable length of time, his judgments will be crude and impulsive as he has little frame of reference within the area of his interest. Where personality shows through, he should be able to make judgments about the character of the authors he reads – this will be a great help to him. He will one day find an idol, only to throw him to the dogs later on. He will begin in one direction, only to reverse it the next day. His emotions will be involved, so that, when he has a bitter experience in his learning, he may be repelled from learning, even suspend it; and, when one conclusion tends to be leading to another which verifies it, he will glow with enthusiasm. But the first months to the first year or so may be a time of little success, filled with much wasted time and many disillusionments, which can be partially attributed to such things as capitalism and freedom of speech, for they are responsible for putting every kind of book in the marketplace, including many that have little or no value.

Since this young adult knows the feeling of progress, he is equipped to sense when things are going well. This is a tremendous asset. His intuitions can save him years of time and, in the long run, can direct him with astounding sensibility toward substantial achievements. But this is only because he has protected his instincts from being exploited, and his individuality and identity from being invaded and disoriented by the demands and expectations of authoritative and controlling persons or institutions.

Ideally, he will try to approach his goal or goals within his field from as many different angles as possible, to avoid treating one small room of his field as the entire house; one of the worst kinds of traps, and about the hardest to have to confront.

In thinking about his motives and objectives in entering his field, he will constantly adapt his studies accordingly. In doing so, he will make many subtle studying decisions, each of which can have a great impact in the end. For example, if he knows that he wants to find cures for diseases, he will focus more on causes of disease than on perfecting common medical procedures. His initial goals and objectives, in this way, begin to blossom or may even become altered as he exercises them within the realities he confronts in his chosen area of interest.

Rather than assume patterns of investigation, he will look for them to be indicated. This is truly the scientist's mode of operation. It is an obvious extension of trying to come to terms with the meaning of things.

It is hoped that he will try to draw up his own philosophy of learning, and philosophy of specified activity along the lines of his interests within his area of study. The successful development of these philosophies, in connection with their actual usefulness and flexibility, is the best means of finding a true footing and maintaining it on increasingly delicate ground as he moves forward in his learning.

Themes of study, major and minor, trends of awareness, and a listing of relevant conclusions, should be the issue of each day's work. However, if the feels bogged down in analysis, he may discard this method of operation for awhile in favor of an impulsive bout of haphazard delving and reading, for his

47

emotions, too, are an educated part of him.

This person will rely on his own observations and decisions to guide him in his learning; and, whenever they cannot do the job, he will sharpen them. He may listen carefully to the advice of teachers, mentors and authoritites in his field; but he will listen more carefully to his own analysis and judgment. He is the ultimate type of student, as he is fully equipped in that capacity. If the whole world around him falters, he will still be a thoroughly competent student. His approach and attitude will carry him through.

THE TEACHER-STUDENT RELATIONSHIP

The teacher is the servant of the student. Whatever the student is to become, it is out of himself that he must become it; which means that he must evolve. He must evolve naturally as a plant or tree evolves, growing up gradually and out of the material that is already him. Consequently, instruction by the teacher, if it is to be appropriate to the needs of the student, must occur in sensitive relationship to where the student is at in his or her thinking, feeling and being.

People are universally the same in their basic psychological, emotional and biological needs, experience many similar obstacles in growing up, and are similarly challenged by existing human conditions; but vary tremendously in their living conditions and circumstances, pattern of development, preferences of association, thought processes, philosophical beliefs, and manner of doing things. A teacher must have an accurate knowledge of the emotional and psychological need systems of the human being, a good knowledge of local and national conditions, and she must teach within the framework of that knowledge; but her teaching becomes applicable to a particular student in connection with the differences to which I have just referred. It is toward these differences that the teacher must direct herself if she is to have any hope of teaching effectively.

The teacher has the responsibility to those whom she would have as her students to find out where each one is at insofar as these differences are concerned. Perhaps the best way of accomplishing this is simply getting to know each other by means of comfortable vehicles, such as doing things together that both teacher and student enjoy, and talking about things of common interest. After the teacher feels she knows where a particular student is at, according to the differences commonly found in people, keeping in mind the phase of development he is in, her next job is to formulate a program of instruction for the student. This should consist of the best of what she, the teacher, has to offer insofar as it can be applied to the learning needs of the student. Once this has been satisfactorily accomplished, at least to the point at which a teacher feels she has some ground for proceeding in attempting to instruct a particular student, the teacher must always guard the sanctity of the point of intended departure. That is, she should never let her method of instruction or choice of subject matter violate the student's learning needs. While it seems incorrect to discourage a teacher from trying to change a student in the areas in which he or she has obvious need for improvement, the teacher must keep in mind that such attempts should be only a small portion of her relating to the student; for her job is not primarily to change students, but to *assist them* in their efforts at changing and improving themselves. The role of assisting the student comprises many different functions: encouraging, sympathizing, challenging, presenting new things, being an example, advising, depending on the changing needs of the particular student. The teacher must be flexible to the student's changing needs, and the classroom situation must be structured with this in mind.

As the teacher has certain teaching requirements placed on her by truth itself, truth places certain learning requirements on the person who wishes to be a student. It is up to the student to earn his self-respect as a student, and to earn respect as a student from anyone he would have as his teacher. The student should not expect a teacher to remain interested in him as a student if she does not respect his efforts as a student. A student who is not making an effort to motivate himself at, and formulate a direction in, his learning activities deserves little respect from a teacher or from himself (insofar as his capacity as student is concerned); because the goal of better self-direction is the foremost purpose of learning. The students most dedicated to learning to guide and direct themselves in their studies and life, and the students most accomplished at guiding and directing themselves in their studies and life, are the students who most inspire themselves to continue learning and who most inspire their teachers to give them all the assistance they can.

Just as the student has privileges in the teacher-student relationship – namely, the privilege of being related to by the teacher according to his unique development as an individual and specific learning needs; and the privilege of *selecting his own subject matter to be learned and his own learning procedure* (I'll elaborate on this proposition in subsequent sections of this treatise.); the teacher has privileges in the teacher-student relationship. Those privileges are to teach what she wants, as she wants and when she wants, so long as she is not in violation of the student's individual learning needs and freedom of choice in doing so; and to teach whom she wants. In other words, she is servant only to the psychological and emotional make-up, living circumstances and basic freedoms of the students she chooses to teach, not to anyone other than those students; and, so long as she walks along this path in connection with those whom she chooses to teach, she need walk along no other path in her teaching.

THINKING FOR ONESELF

It is apparent that teachers, and those who intend to be good students, need to be proficient at thinking; a process commonly referred to as: *thinking for oneself*. It is less apparent, but equally true, that all the rest of us need to be proficient in the art of *thinking for oneself* if we are to lead happy and successful lives.

The average person has to deal with at least some problems in his or her own life every day; not necessarily always different problems, for some may be of an ongoing variety. I am not referring to trivial problems, like what color shirt to wear, or where to dine for supper. I am referring to problems we have in understanding, communicating, living harmoniously, fulfilling day to day needs and accomplishing long-range objectives. The key to solving problems, or handling them as well as can be expected, is thinking; or, to be more precise: *thinking for oneself.*

A person who is accomplished at thinking for himself is one who, with consistent success, applies thought unassisted to enable things to be understood and utilized. It's easy to say, but difficult to accomplish.

In every situation, or set of circumstances, there are things of more and less significance, and the selection of possible responses and possible actions that may be undertaken within that situation or set of circumstances are enormous. A person who thinks for himself can sort through alternatives and possibilities, and will wind up being able to relate to things intelligently and being able to proceed appropriately. He can do so because he has learned how to seek out and find the reality behind the appearances of things. This ability to get to the very bottom of things, or to see the very essence of things, is at the heart of being able to think for oneself.

A person who is successful at thinking for himself tends to take positions in thought and deed. He tends to put things in motion, slow their motion (not by a sluggish presence, but by pitting himself against their thrust), or increase their momentum. Due to his skill at assessing things and understanding them, his life can be very well organized; and his actions and behavior can be timely and appropriate within the context of the events and conditions going on around him. Only because he sees things clearly, and understands them, is it possible for him to act with dexterity and power in his relationship to all the things he is confronted with in his daily life. The combined efforts of many people may not create a result equivalent to the result produced by his effort alone. This is because the thinking of a lot of people is diluted by inner conflicts and uncertainty, which interferes with their ability to follow a clear and definite program over the long term.

A person who is skilled at thinking for himself is nature's prodigy. He learns by watching nature in himself, in others; and in all things both near him and far away. All the laws of life are natural laws and can be observed. The basis of all knowledge and science is, simply, nature.

If a person thinks for himself, truly, he will have the greatest potential for doing anything which life requires of him, or he requires of himself. Yet, if a person cannot think for himself, no skill, no ability and no assistance will be sufficient to enable him to manage his own life wisely and effectively. Being able to think for oneself is so essential that it is behind most of what is done well. Furthermore, the degree to which a thing is done well is likely a result of the degree to which a person can think for himself.

But you may disagree with me. You may argue that a person does not have to think for himself to do many things, such as things he already knows how to do, or things he does naturally. If this is what you believe, you will surely feel that you do not have to think for yourself to pick up a chair, as you already know how to do it. However, imagine that the chair is in a crowded restaurant, possibly reserved for someone who is soon to return; and you are eyeing the chair for the purpose of moving it to a vacant, free-standing table, from which the chairs have been removed, so that you may sit down and eat your lunch. Before you pick up the chair for the purpose of moving it to the nearby table, you will have to think about how it will affect the person who may soon return. In other words, you will have to weigh the pros and cons of picking up the chair. After weighing the pros and cons, you may decide that picking up the chair, in this instance, would probably result in an angry search for the unconscionable chair thief. As a result, it is feasible that you may elect not to pick up the chair after all. If the chair is in the home of a wealthy person, and is valued as an antique, picking it up to move it into another room where a conversation is ongoing, and there is a shortage of seating, might disturb the residents; and, consequently, *thinking for*

53

oneself might be required to avoid an unpleasant confrontation with the residents. Or, perhaps you are thinking of picking up a chair so you can move it to a spot near an old girlfriend who you have just spotted sitting alone at a restaurant table set up for one, which has no additional seating in place. In this instance, you may have to think through many old feelings about your previous relationship with her before getting up the courage to pick up the chair so that you can place it next to her and sit down.

The point of these examples has been to show that there is simply no such thing as picking up a chair, nor doing anything, in a vacuum. There are always reasons for doing things and consequences for having done them. And, in coping with these, it is very often necessary to be able to think for oneself, sometimes extensively, even when performing the most simple of tasks, such as picking up a chair.

Certainly, you can see by my examples that the need to think for oneself shows itself everywhere, and with great frequency, even when attempting the most simple task; and you can see that sensible living is quite impossible without having arrived at some ability in the art of *thinking for oneself.*

Another of the incorrect beliefs concerning thinking is: *If a person has acquired a lot of facts, information and knowledge, he is automatically able to think for himself well, and effectively.*

It sounds plausible; but, in reality there is much more to the process of *thinking for oneself* than that. Having a lot of facts, information and knowledge simply does not guarantee a person can think for himself, either well or effectively. And that is because thinking does not come from a part of a person; nor from certain knowledge that he has, nor from a particular area of knowledge he is well versed in. Thinking is: *the ability of a person to conceptualize and understand as a whole and complete person participating in a whole and complete world.* When a person attempts to think for himself without having a thorough understanding of himself, and a comprehensive grasp of what is important in life, and how best to function successfully, morally and productively within our world; the results of his trying to think for himself will fall far short of what will be required of him in life, even though he may be knowledgeable in some ways, or have a lot of expertise in one particular field or another. *Thinking for oneself*, then, refers to an ability that must be developed and mastered by a whole and complete person, who does not have a narrow and limited focus, and whose thinking skills are not limited to a single subject or to particular things he knows about. All of life must be the schoolroom, and all the essential things that make up life must be the subject matter, of someone who is going to one day be able to think for himself well and effectively. A person must always strive for a *total view of the total picture* if his thinking is one day to have a semblance of what is truly profound and meaningful in life. A person who thinks for himself well and effectively is, indeed, someone who has learned to understand himself, other people, and the things of importance within his immediate environment and within the larger picture of the world as a whole. Going one step further, if the person who is good at thinking for himself is also to be a good person, he must be motivated to apply his awareness and understanding effectively for the betterment of others.

As you can see, *thinking for oneself* is a skill that is not easily accomplished. It is certainly not something one just happens upon; nor is it entirely a natural instinct. The potential for being able to think for oneself may be a natural instinct; but before it can be said of a person that he is good at thinking for himself, his ability at thinking for himself must have undergone a tremendous amount of development. As one does not become an expert mountain climber on his first journey up a mountain, one is not, because he attempts to think for himself, automatically skilled at doing so.

Next, I'd like to present a set of prerequisites I have come up with that I feel are necessary if a person is to be able to think for himself successfully. First of all, a person must have a mind with *intelligent contents*. If he doesn't have very much good information, nor an abundance of meaningful life-experiences, to refer to and draw from, he is going to be ill-equipped to think for himself. As a race cannot be run well by a runner who is in poor health, good thinking cannot be done by a mind that has few concepts, ideas and awarenesses of value. Next, those contents must be *well-integrated* so that the mind will be permitted to work in a coordinated manner. Isolated and unconnected bits of information and facts, and life-experiences that we have never fully comprehended or integrated into our overall view of things, are not helpful to us; and are really no more than a lot of excess baggage that is cumbersome and burdensome to us. Just as, for the purpose of driving a car, one's eyes, ears and hands must all be synchronized; to be good at *thinking for oneself*, the contents of one's mind must all be integrated and coordinated, so that the mind can apply itself in a synchronized manner. Now if a person has these two qualities of mind: intelligent contents, and integration and coordination of those contents, it is still necessary that he have *supportive circumstances* for using his mind, and that he have clarity and soundness of thinking procedure, if he is to succeed at thinking for himself.

In connection with the idea of supportive circumstances, may I say that I consider it a truism that a person will think about things only to the extent that he can retain *faith* that his understanding will thereby increase, and that this increased understanding is something he can exercise within his circumstances, or within circumstances that are conceivably accessible to him. And, conversely, if a person cannot retain faith that his understanding will increase by thinking about things, or if he cannot believe that he can obtain the circumstances necessary to act upon increased understanding, he will have little desire to think about things seriously. I am trying to point out that even thinking, itself, is subject to the most practical considerations; and that a person's *current thinking ability* may not necessarily be an indication of his *true potential* to think for himself successfully or effectively. A person who sees himself hopelessly trapped in obligations or circumstances beyond his control will not begin to exercise his thinking capacity, even if it is excellent. Likewise, a person whose mind has been lying idle for a long time may become a fireball of inventiveness and competency with the incentive of a single plan or idea. If we want to be sure people will apply their minds; that is, try to think for themselves about things, we must show them how it can benefit them. Once they have a clear enough and strong enough reason for thinking, we can rest assured that they will try very hard to think through even the most complex problems and circumstances, and that they will try very hard to guide their lives according to decisions based on depth and thoroughness of thought.

If a person is lacking certain insights, ideas or talents needed for proficiency in thinking, it may be said that he is his biggest obstacle in attempting to think for himself well and effectively. If you are such a person, be consoled that each of us was at one time a poor thinker. No child begins life by being good at thinking for himself. If trying to improve your ability at thinking for yourself seems frustrating at first, and seems to be yielding little beneficial results; be aware that this will change vastly for the better as you put yourself on a path of self-improvement. Each of us is the pair of glasses through which we see things and think about them, and as we improve ourselves – mentally, emotionally and morally – we are improving the prescription of the pair of glasses through which we see things and think about them; and our ability to think for ourself well and effectively will improve proportionately.

The raw material for *thinking for oneself* is points of reference. Points of reference are ideas or feelings about things. They are the things we think about, talk about, experiment with, observe, feel or react to in trying to get somewhere, do something or figure things out. It seems to me that people are often in the position of wishing to find additional points of reference, but are often dissatisfied with the results, or cannot arrive at even partially satisfactory results. Of course, oftentimes there is a lack of awareness of the need for additional points of reference.

Those who are flexible with their points of reference, (meaning that they can view them from different angles, alter them or discard them when appropriate); and, at the same time, committed to seeking additional and more meaningful points of reference, will have the most material to select from in attempting to think for themselves. Developing one's understanding in any area of knowledge, or about any facet of life, or developing any skill can only be done by finding additional points of reference; or, of course, by focusing in better on the ones we already have. Learning to drive a car, for instance, is the process of accumulating points of reference about driving a car. Even those people who don't know how to drive have some points of reference about driving cars that enable them to have a head start on the matter. They know the speed a car should go (one point of reference). They know that a car has a steering wheel to steer it, a gas pedal to increase or decrease the speed, and brakes to stop it (three more points of reference). They know that a car must stop at red lights and move forward on green lights (two more points of reference). Now, in learning to drive car, they will learn facts and techniques or methods; and these facts and techniques or methods consist of, simply, more points of reference. A student driver will learn to maintain a safe distance from the cars in front of him, and he will be taught what is meant by safe distance at various speeds (more points of reference). He will be taught to look into the rear view mirror when slowing to a stop (another point of reference). He will be taught to check the tires to see if the tread is good, to make sure the windshield wipers are good and in working order; he will be taught to enter a freeway at a certain speed (all points of reference). He will be taught how to park; how to signal turns, change lanes, merge with traffic and slow to a stop (more points of reference). In learning these additional points of reference, he is learning about driving a car; and, as the number of points of reference relevant to his driving a car increase in his awareness, his skill at driving a car increases.

Similarly, lifestyle, behavior, perception, involvement, every form of action and thought are a result of the points of reference a person has; and the particular circumstances a person is in, or has access to, in which to make use of those points of reference. As relevant points of reference increase in quality and quantity, the potential to change circumstances, and to prosper from current circumstances and put them to productive use, becomes increasingly available. While this is clear in the example of learning to drive a car, it is not as obvious in learning to live a healthy, happy, aware and productive life; but it is nonetheless equally applicable. Consequently, those who do not find they are getting out of life, or putting into life, what they want to or what they should, had better consider increasing their points of reference, or improving the quality of usage of their current points of reference, so that they will have more or better material to work with in thinking about altering their current circumstances, or putting them to better use.

Points of reference can come from conversation, experiences, thinking, feeling, reactions, observation, experimentation, books or other media outlets: newspapers, television, radio and so forth. But one's own thoughts, feelings, reactions, observations, conversations, experiences and experiments are perhaps the most lucrative in acquiring new points of reference because it is with them that the person tunes in, so to speak. It is with one's own thoughts, feelings, reactions, observations, conversations, experiences and experiments that a person can make the most accurate, integrated and multifaceted connections with things, as they occur on the person's own ground and on his own terms. A person can read an excellent book that has nothing to do with his needs or his circumstances, for example; consequently, the book would be of little value to him. Whereas, if a person simply thinks, feels, reacts, observes, converses, experiences, and sets up his own experiments; he is going to be dealing with the kinds of things that pertain to and concern him.

Now I am not trying to say that having various information, subjects and areas of study that are completely foreign to us, or that we have little interest in, thrust upon us by parents, teachers, schools, our supervisors at work, or by the demands of everyday life, is not worthwhile; for, sometimes we may benefit from it greatly. But, a lot of the time, it is far superior to let a person seek his own points of contact, and find his own things to become involved in, because we can then at least be assured that there is a legitimate reason for the person to be connected and involved with them.

Perpetually exposing a student to things in behalf of the inclinations or judgment of others, which is a common practice in most of our schools, falls extremely short of the ideal, as it is far more important to expose him most frequently to *his own* feelings, reactions, thoughts, observations, conversations, experiences, and experiments; a process truly secure only when promoted by the student's own initiative. The danger of a learning regime established by others, in which the student is expected to adhere faithfully to the rules and expectations of others, such as teachers, parents or school administrators, is that the entire learning process is then being foisted upon the student without reference to his needs, wants or natural inclinations. This practice, not surprisingly, may result in a justified and bitter resentment toward the learning process; and, if much learning takes place under the guidelines and auspices of such a method of teaching, it may well be unfortunate that it has, because such teaching may produce in a student an alienation from all that is natural and true for him or her. It is apparent to me that bitterness and resentment toward learning, and alienation from oneself, are greatly fostered and encouraged by the very educational process that is most often promoted and adhered to within our schools.

Having discussed the raw material for thinking for oneself, which I referred to as points of reference, I would like to present my thoughts on the subject of deciding what it is we shall think for ourselves about. Here are five things that I feel a person should ask himself about something he is considering thinking for himself about, if he is to do so effectively and in a way that is true for him. In honestly answering these five questions, a person can at least have a yardstick for measuring and evaluating the suitability of things he wishes to think for himself about.

(1) Is it a thing of good quality?

(2) Does it apply to me? (Is it really something I can constructively identify with?)

(3) Am I prepared to think for myself about it at this time?

(4) Is its form of presentation the one I can best relate to in thinking for myself about it?

(5) How should I approach thinking for myself about it?

In deciding if something is a thing of good quality, one must first be able to sense its presence. This can be done through a methodical reasoning process, or simply by using one's gut level feelings. Next, one has to isolate it from the material with which it is associated or commingled. In isolating something, one may find that he has only a part of a thing; in which case, the rest of it would have to be constructed. In isolating a thing, one may find that it is in damaged form; in which case, it would have to be repaired. In isolating a thing, one may find that he has only the raw material for something; in which case, it would have to be built or formed out of the raw material. After something has thus been isolated in its complete form, or isolated and then turned into its complete form, one is able to ask the question, "Is it a legitimate thing, a real thing?" Once it is determined that the thing isolated is in its complete form, and is also a legitimate thing, a real thing, one is finally in a position to try to ascertain its actual quality. The quality of a piece of information or knowledge is determined by measuring its usefulness and applicability to the human situation.

In asking oneself the question, "Does it apply to me?" it is, of course, necessary for a person to have a good sense of himself; that is, of his values, preferences, interests and capabilities. If a person has a good idea of what he is, and knows what the thing he is considering consists of – as determined by question (1), he should have no problem in deciding to what extent it applies to him. But if the person is vague about his own essence, or about the essence of the thing he is considering, I see no way of determining to what extent the thing applies to him.

As to question (3), it is of course plausible that while something really does apply to a person, the person is just not ready to become involved with it. This could be for countless, varying reasons: circumstances, state of mind, things of prior importance, etc. In such a situation, the person must decide if he will file the thing away for future review or if he will let it slip away into the oblivion of forgotten memories.

As to question (4), things can be in countless different forms. The form of a thing that is good for one person to relate to may not be the form of it that is good for another person to relate to. In buying wall paint, for example, one person may want blue, while another wants yellow. Both may be buying the same brand of wall paint, but they each want it in a different form. The same type of thing occurs where things to be thought about are concerned. If a thing applies to a person, and he is ready to think for himself about it, he may find its form not to his taste or not suitable to his needs. So he should alter it to a more suitable form before proceeding with it. For example, suppose the thing that was isolated was the statement that Napoleon was an interesting man. "Interesting man" can be put into many different forms for the convenience of the person who is thinking about it: brilliant, groovy, well-rounded, colorful despite his wickedness, and so on. A person should alter the fact into the form that best suits him before thinking for himself about why it is so, what he shall do with the information, etc.

As to question (5), as the form of something may vary, so may one's approach to it. Approach can encompass things such as how frequently one will associate with it, toward what end, what one will associate it with, etc. In *thinking for oneself* about something, result has a great deal to do with approach. For example, if a person picks the wrong purpose for thinking about something that really does apply to him, I do not see how the results could be positive. Likewise, if he associates with it too little or too much, the result cannot be as good as it should be.

I have now described some of the misconceptions about *thinking for oneself*, some of the conditions most favorable for *thinking for oneself*, and some of the component parts of *thinking for oneself*. To the component parts of *thinking for oneself*, I would like to add the following information: If *thinking for oneself* is to be properly undertaken, it must be a serious endeavor. It must be undertaken autonomously, and not while one is in the grip of the persuasive influences of other people nor while one is trying to satisfy the expectations of other people. It must be undertaken without bias; in other words, without prejudging or predetermining the results. It must be done in a thorough manner, assessing all relevant data; and a true spirit of scientific inquiry must prevail. This means that one must be willing to discover that the opposite of his tentative or initial assessment of a matter, and the opposite of a long-cherished belief, will prevail.

I hope that this essay will encourage students and educators to give more importance to learning to *think for oneself*, and less importance to the accumulation of information, facts and skills. For, although the accumulation of information, facts and skills is important, as long as they pertain to a student's interests and needs; they are useless in the hands of someone who cannot think for himself. I also hope this essay can encourage those people who are not educators or students to acquire a proficiency at *thinking for oneself*, if they have not done so already; because a proficiency at *thinking for oneself* can vastly improve each person's ability to make life a meaningful, productive and rewarding experience.

THREE TASKS

There are many things a youngster must learn if he is going to become a capable adult. Reading, writing and basic math skills are essential, as everyone knows. But being skilled at reading, writing and basic math do not equip a student to find his way in the world. For this purpose, becoming accomplished at three tasks will give him a good start at being able to conduct himself successfully in the world. Those three tasks are inherited by each student, and must be mastered if a student is to move forward in life in a meaningful way. They are:

(1) To learn to observe for the purpose of understanding the true content and meaning of things. (I referred to this in the section on THINKING FOR ONESELF.)

(2) To develop a worthwhile concept of the meaning of life to him.

(3) To learn to maneuver well in his environment.

Fulfilling task number one indicates balance, fulfilling number two indicates direction, and fulfilling number three indicates mobility. I shall now elaborate on each of these three tasks in the order first presented.

To accomplish task (1), a person must attempt to observe things *accurately* and *thoroughly*. This is the very first task a thinking person must undertake who wishes to keep his feet firmly planted on the road to understanding and enlightenment. If a person cannot properly analyze and understand what he perceives, of what good is he as a student of ideas, information or even skills? A person should try to perfect his perceptual skills before attempting any fast or efficient acquisition of information, skills or ideas. A person should not try to master things that are extremely complex before his perceptual skills have proven themselves in connection with the things to be found in his personal circumstances and immediate environment.

Accurate and *thorough* observing is a form of studying, but it is a process far different from the process of studying that is common in most of our schools. *Accurate and thorough* observing is the process of studying things in great depth. Such observing is a one-to-one encounter with something without distractions. It is dynamic. The rules of the encounter are created by the observer and the observed. It is going on a private adventure with something. It is getting inside of

63

something and finding a whole world vibrant with possibilities. You lift the thing up and look at it, in the dark, in the sunlight, in cold weather, in hot weather. You drop it, throw it. You ponder it from a hundred different angles. You become its ever-watchful friend. In time, it begins to reveal to you its essence as if it were rewarding you.

Since such observing is an attempt to account for something in its entirety, it is oftentimes a slow moving and sparsely happening process, though nonetheless dynamic, until one manages his way into the heart of an issue or phenomenon. It consists of sifting and comparing and measuring and experimenting for as long as may be necessary. This type of activity requires a certain habit of mind far unlike the habits of mind fostered by contemporary studying requirements. Contemporary students are encouraged to flit and fly from one idea to the next, from one assignment to the next and from one lecture room to the other. They have little time to inspect a thing closely, to really become absorbed in it. They are taught not to be in-depth observers. They are taught that examining things in great depth wastes time and is a hindrance to getting things done.

All the things a person will do will be done within the context of his concept of the meaning of life, which brings me to an elaboration of task (2). If a person's concept of the meaning of life is a drab one that does not inspire him, or if his concept of the meaning of life simply confuses him, his learning will resemble the movement of a train heading somewhere without any tracks along which to travel. Once a person begins to formulate a worthwhile concept of the meaning of life that he is able to relate to and proceed from with comfort and satisfaction, his life begins to have for him a full significance. Then he can try to represent his concept of the meaning of life in his thoughts and deeds; in other words, he can try to act on what he knows, as he now has a valid framework in which to do so. Further learning will include improving his concept of the meaning of life; and learning to represent it in the direction of his studies, and in his thoughts and deeds. Learning that occurs out of the context of one's concept of the meaning of life takes place as so much deadweight, and competes with a person's identity, sensitivity and integrity. A student's development and studies must, from the very first and thereafter, be geared in every respect toward his developing and acting upon a worthwhile concept of the meaning of life.

Task (3), maneuvering well in one's environment, is possible only if a person has a *participating knowledge* of what his environment consist of, and how to make the best use of it. It is actually one step beyond observing. It is making observations work for you in applied situations; but, it is more, for it is also having enough correct observations about the important elements in your environment to enable you to handle your entire environmental circumstances with a skill which approximates success. (By environment is meant: the environment common to all human beings and the local environment common to the people in your town or city.)

MOVING THE ENTIRE PERSON FORWARD

What is ordinarily considered higher education: college and university level, should be peopled with individuals who are becoming accomplished at tasks one, two and three. This is the minimum with which education can proceed on an adult level. Without some proficiency at these three tasks, a person is still a cripple, and will become but an educated cripple if he attempts to move forward in his education without their assistance. Prior to achieving some proficiency at these three tasks, reaching for sophisticated learning goals and objectives brings to mind an amateur swimmer who has assigned himself the task of swimming the Atlantic. And this is not an overstatement. Having a mind that works well in certain areas, or at certain ideas or skills, but is not proficient in the various tasks and responsibilities that life requires of us all (among which are tasks one, two and three), can be compared to being a rich man who is surrounded by robbers. It is like continually acquiring money that is continually being stolen. What good is it to brag about the beauty of the paintings in one's house if one's house has no roof? What good is it to start on a trip at a time when one has just taken ill? In the end, the money will be gone, the paintings will be ruined and the trip will be a failure. If a man has a car, he does not attend only to the tires and disregard the rest of the car. If he wants to have a car that works, he attends equally to all its essential working parts. He knows that it is of little significance to have a transmission in perfect working condition if the engine is faulty. He knows that a perfect engine and transmission are insignificant if the battery is on its last legs; and that if any one of many hundreds of parts ceases to work, the car is useless. It is the same with living. If a man has the ability to do something, but cannot find the desire, the ability is worthless. If a man cannot sort out his life so that he is at peace with himself, his talents and desire will be hindered. If a man does not know what to do with his free time, the time that is not free will be affected. If a man has a lot of difficulty using one of his emotions, all the man's strength will be chained to that weakness. He cannot run because a part of him barely knows how to crawl. If a man loses part of his respect for himself, the fact that he is able may be of little consequence; as he may avoid the effort necessary to succeed

66

because of his attitude toward himself. It seems that it takes only one little plug to let out the entire bath water.

Does a man move forward with his feet, and leave his arms behind? Such a man would be absurd! It is equally absurd for a man to move forward in engineering, law, medicine, skill at business, or whatever, without moving forward in all aspects of life.

Let us, then, establish that a person who is excellent at something is not for this to receive final praise. Not until a study has been made of his degree of competency at the rest of life, with the results showing an excellence there also, will he be fully congratulated. Let us also establish that the idea in education is to move the *entire person* forward. To move the entire person forward, a total approach to living is required. We need to know what the important requirements are for living a full and responsible life; and, above all else, encourage the student toward a mastery of those requirements. The key in accomplishing this is getting to know and understand oneself, people in general, one's environment and circumstances, the ways of the world, and the various values and principles which add meaning and purpose to life. For, if one has a good understanding of these things, he will then be able to see what is required of him to function smoothly, meaningfully and productively in life, and to progress in whatever direction he chooses.

In getting to understand oneself, people in general, one's environment and circumstances, the ways of the world, and the various values and principles which add meaning and purpose to life, one has to seek answers to hundreds of different questions, questions such as the following ones. "What types of people should I associate with? How much of my time should I spend engaged in social activities, relaxation and having fun? If I don't like a person, must I tell that person so – is that one of the things that is meant by honesty? To what extent should I allow compassion to motivate me; and at what points can I turn away from the needs of others so that I may attend to my own needs? How long can I remain idle, and without purpose, before I should feel warned? Is doing nothing at all a therapeutic form of existence with many hidden potentials? What are the virtues of capitalism, of socialism? What are the things of most importance in life? What are the things I need to be happy from day to day? Who are the persons, living or dead, most worthy of emulation? Does every person fall in love

67

at least once in their lifetime, and is it necessary to fall in love in order to live a happy life? Are the local living conditions and circumstances which the average person confronts from day to day of sufficient quality to enable him or her to have a fair opportunity to live a wholesome, happy and productive life?"

As you can see, learning to understand all that is necessary in order to live a full and responsible life is a truly complicated job. It is so complicated that only a wide range of experience, a great deal of examining, analyzing and evaluating, and a great willingness to seriously consider beliefs and opinions which differ from one's own, can permit one the opportunity of succeeding at it.

Teachers should assist students in this most important undertaking by making sure that their teaching is aimed at advancing the awareness and ability of the total person. Ordinarily, education in our country is not concerned with the student's development as a total person. This becomes obvious when one considers the fact that students are not tested or graded in their skills or knowledge insofar as they affect the development of the total person.

In evaluating the learning progress of the total person, as opposed to the learning progress of a part of the person (such as their memory), many concerns arise which are usually not considered to be relevant to the learning process, such as:

(1) Are the student's motives for learning clear in his own mind?

(2) Is the student ready for more learning, or should other things precede it?

(3) Is the student picking the right things to learn?

(4) Is the student internalizing the things he is learning in a healthy way?

(5) Does the student find enough applications for what he is learning, so that he is truly living it; or is his learning a stagnant part of him, therefore an irritant in his life?

In looking at the progress of the total person with such ideas in mind, one may discover any number of things. It may be found that a student is undergoing some anxiety or other; and, rather than add to the confusion, his mind should first be put in order, however long it may take, before further learning occurs. It may be found that the student is particularly lacking in an area of life that has nothing to do with what he is studying; and he should first attend to that inadequacy. It may be found that a student's motives for acquiring certain knowledge are unclear in his mind, which would mean that the knowledge would be learned in a faulty fashion. Therefore, the student would have to attend to clarifying his motives before continuing his other learning activities. It may be found that a student is learning much that is unnecessary for him to learn, thereby wasting his time and crowding his life with that which is superfluous to it. It may be that he adapts better to a different method of learning or to different learning conditions. It may be that his desire to learn is not strong enough, and would therefore have to be investigated; that it would be more important for him to investigate it than to continue his other learning activities.

If this very personal approach to education, which is necessary if education is to represent the forward movement of the entire person, is to be implemented, a host of additional realizations must be documented for the purpose. The rest of this treatise will consist of pertinent additional realizations that have occurred to me.

THE NECESSITY TO ASSOCIATE IN A POSITIVE MANNER

Next, I'd like to present the concept: "It is necessary for a person to associate with things in a manner that affects him or her in a positive way; in other words, in a way that constitutes *a positive life experience*."

There is a school of thought which theorizes that human beings are tough, or should be; and that they should be able to make sacrifices, endure hardships, make compromises and adapt to all sorts of conditions and circumstances that are unfriendly to their nature. While it is true that people can adapt to many different kinds of situations and circumstances, it is also true that human nature is sensitive and fragile in many ways; and when a person accepts, or adapts to, an uncomfortable situation or set of circumstances, it eventually takes a toll on his well-being and peace of mind.

Why wait for the inevitable to happen? Why wait for disintegration, collapse, illness, depression or misery? When we understand the conditions and circumstances which favor human well-being, happiness and progress, we must insist upon them. Though we may not always be able to have what we want, or what we seek, still we should never completely accept what we know to be alien to our nature.

There are three good indicators that can be used to determine if the learning experiences of students in our schools constitute "positive life experiences;" or if they are, in fact, alien to human nature. When the three indicators are adhered to, the educational experience is beneficial; and when they are abandoned, the educational experience is suspect. These three indicators will seem ill-conceived and incorrect to those who have been trained that the primary responsibility of a student is to do what educators tell him to do. The three indicators are:

(1) Focusing: The freedom to choose what one will focus one's attention on within the learning process.

(2) Self-identification: The freedom to choose what one will become personally associated with in the learning process.

(3) Procedure: The freedom to choose how one will proceed in becoming personally associated or involved with things within the learning process.

If a person, for whatever reason, chooses to put his foot in one direction or on a certain spot when he is walking, we realize that no one has a right to tell him he cannot. We also realize that if every time a person took a step, he was subjected to the interjection of another's rules for how he should go about doing it, he would soon lose the desire to walk as it would be too burdensome and cumbersome. It is this very feeling of being burdened and encumbered that a student must necessarily feel when there is a steady diet of rules, expectations and guidelines thrust upon him in his learning. And his response to a continual regime of rules, expectations and guidelines in connection with his learning activities must, likewise, include a loss of desire to learn.

It is a strange fact that although loss of desire to learn should occur in proportion equal to the intensity and extent of imposed rules, directives and expectations, just as in the case of being told where to put your feet when you are walking, loss of desire to learn does not necessarily cause a person to cease participating in the learning process. People may actively participate in the learning process while having lost a good deal, or all, of their desire to learn. They do not then, of course, participate in a constructive manner. I believe that this phenomenon is a prolific occurrence in the educational institutions of the world. Education which occurs within the freedom to choose range, as detailed in numbers (1), (2) and (3) earlier in this essay, has the best potential for constructive results. All forms of compulsory education are suspect.

If a person is in the process of reading a book, he may decide he does not want to continue reading it. The reasons may be complex; but right or wrong, complex or simple, they are his reasons and must therefore be respected. If the person is a student trying to pass a course, and must read the book to do so; he will, if he wishes not to read any more of it, be impressed with the fact that the way he feels toward something is not the way he may conduct himself toward it; at least, not in his capacity as student. This can be a cruel lesson with bitter consequences. It is as if he is being told: "It does not behoove your future for you to be yourself." This lesson is drummed into the conscious and unconscious minds of students around the world, daily stabbing into their identity and damaging their free spirit. The student who is often imposed upon by his instructor's requirements of him, and by school policy, must admit to himself that his studies are not in favor of his immediate sense of well-being. He will then construct walls of negative attitudes between himself and his studies, protecting himself from deep involvement with them. He will participate with only one foot or a few toes in, and learn to practice the illusion of involvement to pacify the necessary persons or to conform to prevailing policies, using up much of his time and energy in this worthless maneuver. Or he will take the alternative route, and truly become involved in his studies at the expense of his integrity, causing disrespect for himself and alienation from himself to develop. While he will be doing his studies as expected, he will resent them; and this resentment will eventually break his will as a student, or as a person, or both. Or else, he will remain forever stranded between being unreal as a student and real as a person.

A person breathes at his own rate; he looks where he chooses to look; he sits where he chooses to sit; he speaks when he chooses to speak; he laughs when it suits him; he gets angry when it suits him; he sleeps when it suits him; he says what he wants to say; he responds as he wants to respond; he eats when he wants to eat. What does this tell us? It tells us that it is a fundamental part of being human to be and do what you want, when you want, as you want. This truth holds for every activity a person engages in, including learning.

Would a man build a chair for himself if someone stood behind him, telling him where to hit with a hammer, how and when to swing it with each blow? Of course not! Then why should a person build a life for himself out of being told what books to read, when to read them, what courses to take, what lectures to attend, how to act in the lecture room, what tests to take, when to take them, and so forth?

Let us say, for the purpose of elaborating on my point, that I am a student and must take a history test. I am required to know about a certain war and all the events pertinent to it. In reading assigned books on the subject, I come upon a certain date I know is important to be remembered in connection with that war. I would not simply remember the date as I am supposed to because I am not just a student studying for a test. I am also a person. Anything could run through my mind, perhaps something like:"I have more urgent and more esthetic things to concern myself with than remembering that date. I'll forget it in two weeks anyway. It will block out some other thought that I may prefer to think. I have difficulty seeing the reasons for remembering all those things about the war anyway. I can see that it is nice to know it happened; but, beyond that, what does it have to do with my interests?"

Do you think a person reacting in this way to his studies can benefit from them? Can you see that such reactions will have serious consequences to the student's life if he continues to pursue his studies under the same conditions? There is no student who does not react to his studies. The important thing is to determine how he is reacting. Not just a simple determination, but all the precise feelings and thoughts he has about them. It is only when his reactions to his studies are specifically determined that we can begin to have a true idea of what his studies are doing to him; and that we can begin to see if they are harming him or not. And, remember, pain can be an unconscious phenomenon; hence, first impressions, even the student's own initial responses, are not necessarily to be trusted in this regard.

Don't you think it is time we find out what current studying habits are doing to students? What if, all along, millions of students worldwide have been accumulating negative attitudes toward themselves to the extent that they have become knowledgeable under current educational methods? What if learning by "doing what one is told to do," as is currently the norm in our schools, has all along influenced the student away from a sensitivity to his own nature, and discouraged him from developing into what he is most suited to be; causing him to be a failure, though a success by false standards? I maintain that this has happened to millions of students in schools throughout the world, and is still happening to millions of students.

The idea is for each person to relate to things in a way that suits his nature and state of mind. This is the only truly healthy manner of associating with anything.

An important aspect of this philosophy is that one should relate to things at the point of strongest interest or strongest emotion. Not relating to things at the point of strongest interest or strongest emotion can be compared to playing tennis with one who is far your inferior at the game, or having the ability to leap high fences and being shown only low ones. It just cannot begin to motivate the person to do his best or to find true joy in what he is doing. Methods of instruction contrary to this principle abound in every form of education, ranging from teaching music to instructing employees. To be properly motivated to play the piano, for example, a person should relate to the piano at the point of strongest emotion and most pure feeling. For him to do less is to deny himself contact with himself where he intuitively most desires it, where the piano is

73

concerned. Since it is the esthetics of playing the piano that will turn the person on; he should be motivated to the piano via his esthetic reactions to its sounds, and improve in his ability to play the piano via increasing his esthetic involvement with its sounds. The way piano should be taught, I feel, is to help students become increasingly involved with their esthetic reactions to its sounds, rather than by teaching them just to *replicate sounds* other people have created in the form of compositions, or by ushering them with endless prodding through a stream of totally boring finger exercises. This latter mode of instruction is a dominant practice in piano teaching around the world; and instruction in all the arts, especially the performing arts, is dominated by a similar type of teaching, revealing a dearth of respect for beauty, resulting in an immense destruction of beauty in the hearts of millions of people by careless and foolish persons around the world who think they understand; but do not understand, art.

If a desire to *replicate sounds* on the piano is a product of the student's esthetic involvement with the piano, he will then replicate those sounds he feels motivated to replicate, and in the manner he feels motivated to replicate them. In this way, practicing piano techniques and learning musical compositions become very real and natural endeavors. In this way, the spirit of art is not defiled in the acquiring of technical artistic skills.

Though I am not a musician, I can imagine myself teaching piano using the principles I have formulated. For a literary demonstration of how I would do this, I shall make the subject a little boy named Johnny. Johnny's mother has brought him to his first piano lesson in the instructor's home. The three of them are getting acquainted.

Mother: "I have brought Johnny here because I want him to learn to play the piano."

Instructor: "Does he want to play the piano? Does he know what it can offer him?"

Mother: "I think so."

Instructor: "Come here, Johnny. Let's talk about the piano .... The piano is an instrument through which you can talk about how you feel. If you feel sad, you can show it on the piano. If you feel happy, you can show it on the piano. If you feel angry, you can show that on the piano too. .... You like pretty things, don't you? And fun things? Well, you can create both on the piano simply by touching it in different places. Come, I'll show you." (*Takes boy over to the piano*.) "The things that say what you feel inside of you, and that say pretty and fun things are these things. They're called keys. Try hitting them with your fingers and see what happens. .... If you like doing it, your mother will bring you to me once a week and we can do it together. .... I would like to help you learn how to make it say what you want it to. And I want you to see how it can surprise you and say very nice things you never knew about. The piano can actually teach you, did you know that? But if you want to learn about playing the piano, you must always remember never to play it except when it is your friend. It is fine not to like something, and say it on the piano; but you must never try to speak on the piano, or let it speak to you, when you feel you do not like the piano. The piano is not to hurt you, and you are not to hurt the piano. .... Now, see if you can say something you want to say. See if the sounds you hear excite you. As long as you enjoy making the sounds, you should make them. If you do not enjoy making them, you should stop." (*To mother*): "I wish him to develop a spirited relationship between himself and the keys, independent of me. He and the piano must discover each other. Once I can see they are beginning to get along, I can make suggestions to him as to how I feel he can improve his relationship with the piano; though with this type of instruction, one never knows how the student will react to suggestions from the teacher. Once in awhile, the teacher is left out right from the beginning, and the student and piano guard the privacy of their relationship as intensely as two jealous lovers. If that happens to your child, you will be very lucky, indeed; for it will indicate he has found a method of making the piano work for him: for his feelings, thoughts and needs, which is really what we are after anyway. .... His first few lessons will consist of simply encouraging him to pound away on the keys to his heart's content, and enouraging him to pick out interesting or pleasing sounds. You may not see the wisdom of this; but, I assure you, it is the most dynamic and personal introduction to the piano possible. Later, he and I will work together in discovering a way we can blend the things I have to teach with his learning needs, interests and inclinations. I will always make an effort to teach him the compositions or techniques he will find inspiring, challenging and enjoyable. If his lessons cease to be enjoyable to him; either I am not being a successful teacher or he has become uninterested in what I have to offer; and we will have to reassess our relationship with each other at that time."

QUALITY OF KNOWING

The next thing I would to present on educating the entire person, as opposed to educating simply a part of him, is quality of knowing. Quality of knowing, as I view it, comprises four aspects: bookkeeping, integration of the contents of the mind, application of the contents of the mind to the person's life, and intrinsic quality of the contents of the mind.

(1) *Bookkeeping*: Think about how many different philosophies, beliefs and points of view each of us is exposed to during our lifetime. Many times, those who are proponents of a point of view, or system of beliefs, offer convincing arguments which sway our thinking. And think about how many different moods each of us is inclined to become immersed in, and about the fact that one's thoughts and feelings about things may vary with one's moods. Next, think about how people's opinions and feelings about things can change from time to time as they grow up and mature. Next, consider the fact that people are often unclear about some of their own beliefs, interests or choice of direction in life simply because they have not yet fully decided about them. Lastly, think about the fact that the human mind is constantly acquiring new impressions, new information and new experiences; while forgetting about other impressions, other information and other experiences that it once focused upon. I have asked you to consider these things to enable me to be more convincing in pointing out that the contents of the human mind are tremendously varied, subtle and complex. All this having been said, I hope I have laid a sufficient foundation to introduce two rather incredible concepts for your consideration, which you may have otherwise rejected at the outset. Those concepts are: *If we are to be able to find things in our mind, we must know where we put them; and, if we are to know the use of things in our mind, we must be clear about why we put them there in the first place.*

I'm sure that most people will tend to agree that the mind is the storing place for what we know; and, most will probably agree that the mind is not a trained secretary, automatically organizing and filing incoming ideas, information and impressions for us; nonetheless, most people will think that the concern I have just expressed over where we have put a thing in our mind, or over why we put it in, is unrealistic and doesn't really apply to life. And, I'm sure most people believe that a person never goes wandering around in his mind looking for the place he has put something, and a person never says to himself, "Hmm, now what's that doing in my mind? I wonder why I put it there?"

It is true that people rarely think about the contents of their mind in these terms. But the fact that people do not consciously go wandering in their mind looking for the place they have put something, and do not consciously question the use for things in their mind, does not prove that they have no need to: periodically examine the contents of their mind; and revise, change, reorganize and reclassify those contents. Because the contents of a human mind are of tremendous quantity, and are enormously varied, subtle and complex; I believe that there is no way of keeping up a good rapport with them, or of coping with them, without a highly refined system of organization and great sophistication of definition of those contents. In addition, I believe that we must periodically do a spring cleaning of the contents of our mind, and dispose of much that is no longer needed. When doing that, we must also reorganize, reshape and revise the remaining contents, as needed. A person's mind can be a treasure chest filled with wonderful things, or a junk heap of useless information and inferior opinions, depending upon how skillfully and conscientiously he does his job of being the caretaker of its contents.

(2) *Integration of the contents of the mind*: Since making use of a piece of information or knowledge within our mind is done by our whole mind, it is necessary for what we know to be an integrated part of our mind if our mind is to be able to relate to it effectively. As an aid in showing that this is true, I'd like to ask you, the reader, to accept the proposition that there exists in a particular person's mind a piece of information or knowledge that is quite intact and worthwhile; however, it has not been integrated into the way his particular mind is organized or into the way his particular mind works. Consequently, while the piece of information or knowledge adequately represents something valid and useful, and perhaps something substantial, it is not a usable part of that person's mind. For all practical purposes, then, it is a useless appendage of his mind. Facts, ideas, information, feelings about things, awarenesses, even skills, are all useless to a person until they become integrated into the existing contents of his mind, and into the way his particular mind works. It is essential, then, that the various contents of one's mind be well organized and com-

bined into an integrated way of viewing things and acting upon them; and if they cannot be, they should be forgotten or unlearned.

(3) *Application of the contents of the mind to the person's life*: A person may know things that are legitimate, valid and worthwhile in themselves, yet which do not apply to his life; meaning that they do not apply to who he is, how he thinks, what he does nor how he lives. A person may know things which, though appropriate for someone else to know, are obstacles and impediments in his life. Having unnecessary knowledge, or an excess of knowledge, is just as inappropriate as having poor knowledge or an inadequate amount of knowledge.

If a person plans a trip, he will select clothes, personal effects and other items suitable for the type of trip he has planned. If it is to be a sightseeing trip, he may want a camera. If it is to be a business trip, he may want to bring along his briefcase. If it is to be a trip for therapeutic reasons – to relax his nerves and obtain a measure of peace and quiet, away from the loud and overcrowded city and the bustling and hectic activity of the daily workweek, he may want to bring along a fishing pole and a few good books. But his selection of things to take with him will be different for each different type of trip he has planned. In like fashion, a person should select to learn those types of things that are suitable for the type of mind he has, and the type of life he is in the midst of living, or wishes to live in the not-too-distant future. If the things he is learning do not properly apply to his life, he will one day wake up to find himself ill-prepared for the life he is living, or wishes to live, in spite of all the knowledge he has acquired, even though it may be impressive in content and quality.

In learning, then, we must look not for quantity, nor simply for quality; but for suitability to our own needs, talents and abilities.

(4) *Intrinsic quality of the contents of the mind*: In the eyes of many people, a person who is knowledgeable about many things, and whose mind can be observed to be dexterous and logical, would qualify as having a good mind. However, such a mind may lack certain knowledge that is pertinent to living a sensible and constructive life, and may exhibit flaws in judgment or awareness which become obstacles as circumstances become increasingly sophisticated or complex. In the final analysis, such a mind has contents of inadequate quality.

In measuring the intrinsic quality of the contents of a person's mind, we must also keep in mind that knowing of a thing, or about a thing, is not the same as knowing a significant amount about it; and knowing a significant amount about it is not the same as knowing all about it that should be known about it. It is rare that someone knows all about something, and it is less common than one would suppose that someone knows an adequate amount about something. A person can know an adequate amount about something insofar as it pertains to the limitations of his own abilities and circumstances, but this is not the same as knowing an adequate amount about it. For example, do you know all that it is necessary to know to prevent World War III, or to stop the Aids virus from spreading rapidly? And would less be an adequate amount? Of course not. At best, you may be satisfied that you know an adequate amount about these subjects insofar as your own ability to do something about them is concerned, but this does not mean that you know an adequate amount about them. Does a lawyer ever know enough about the law to be able to figure out how to ensure the greatest amount of justice under any given set of circumstances? Of course not. Then, can he ever be said to know an adequate amount about the law? In my opinion, he cannot. I doubt there are a great many lawyers who can even do a good job of defining justice. "The greatest good for the greatest number" is a commonly offered definition of justice, but in my opinion it can be no more than one of its characteristics. In trying to define justice, there are many things to be considered. For example, do the rights of the individual take precedence over the rights of society? Is justice determined by the kind of revenge we impose upon the wrongdoer, or by the quality of compensation we award the victim, or both? (In my opinion, justice is not complete until the victim of injustice is made whole.) What place does mercy for the criminal play in the concept of justice; and should the wrongdoer be expected to pay with "an eye for an eye," or through public service of some kind? Does a criminal have a right to be rehabilitated at taxpayer's expense by virtue of the fact he is a member of the human race? These are questions that occur to me when thinking about the nature of justice, and are the types of questions I feel must be considered when attempting to define justice. The task becomes even more complex when one is faced with the necessity of making a decision based upon correct principles of justice. If a man kills another, for example, where is there a lawyer with adequate knowledge of justice to be able to calculate for us the really just thing to do about it, all things considered? Who really knows? So let us use the words "knowing" and "knowledge" with all due humility henceforth, if we do not do so already.

PERCEIVING, ORGANIZING AND REVISING THE EXISTING CONTENTS OF ONE'S MIND

The type of person each of us is, as well as the type of behavior each of us will exhibit and the quality of life each of us will live, will to a large extent be determined by the contents of our mind. One of the primary reasons that people live unsuccessful or unhappy lives is that the contents of their minds are in disarray, or are of poor quality. The contents of one's mind can be altered or improved upon so that it better serves its intended purpose; but, before that can occur, the contents must first be clearly identified.

In examining the contents of someone's mind for the purpose of taking an inventory and eventually improving those contents, many different types of evaluations can be made, and many different types of measurements can be taken. If a map is made of the contents of a *normal* or *average* person's mind, streets, towns and cities will not be indicated. Instead, we will find such things as facts, information, simple ideas and complex concepts. We will find feelings about things and impressions of things, some of which are vague or unclear. We will find some prejudices. We will find some partial ideas, some poorly formulated ideas, and some incorrect ideas. We will find patterns of thinking, some of which are sensible and logical, others of which are superficial or pointless. We will find attitudes, and tendencies toward certain moods or states of mind, some of which are healthy; and some of which are detrimental, or in need of improvement. We will find certain personality characteristics; and some automatic patterns of response to things, which may have been learned or acquired over the years. We will find principles, values and beliefs, which form the foundation of the person's character, and determine if the person is honest, ethical, good and kind; or cruel, dishonest corrupt, greedy and wicked; or any combination of these. We will find some contradictory thoughts and some contradictory beliefs. We will find tendencies of thought or habits of thought, and preferences of subject matter upon which the mind selects to focus most frequently. There may be some other categories of things to be found within an *average* or *normal* human mind that I have overlooked.

This listing of the wide array of contents that can normally be found within the human mind surely indicates that a good map of those contents is needed. But does anyone have such a map? Has anyone heard of the existence of such a map? Since no such map can be purchased or found, it is up to each individual to make a map of the contents of his or her mind. However, unlike the contents of a house, the contents of a human mind are often not easy to identify or evaluate. This is in part because the *pair of glasses* through which each of us views the contents of our own mind is prejudiced in our favor. Each of us wants to think that everything within our mind is as it should be; or that only minor changes and improvements in those contents need to be made. But nothing could be further from the truth. One of the main reasons we have a faulty world is because the contents of people's minds are in disarray, or are of poor quality. Educators are partly to blame for the existence of so many poorly educated minds because most educators deal only in imparting collections of facts and information, and not in improving the overall quality of the human minds they are responsible for instructing.

Because the contents of a *normal* or *average* human mind are so varied and can exist in great quantity, identifying and organizing the contents of one's own mind is a lengthy and time consuming task, but worth the effort. I believe that accurately identifying the contents of one's own mind can be satisfactorily accomplished by each person over a period of a few months or longer using pen and paper.The objective would be *not* to list all your thoughts and impressions about things; but to distill the essence of: your beliefs and values; your motives and goals; your personal habits and pertinent psychological and emotional characteristics; your interests, problems, needs and vulnerabilities; your areas of confusion, self-doubt and uncertainty; and any other feelings or thoughts you have that you consider to be essential aspects of the person you are. The entirety of this procedure is the process of self-analysis, and should be regarded as an essential part of everyone's education. If a person can accomplish the task of accurately identifying the contents of his own mind, he will have done himself the greatest service possible; for he will have prepared his mind for learning, growing and expanding. How can one learn, mature or expand one's awareness and understanding of things if one is unclear about the actual contents of one's own mind, or if the contents of one's own mind are vague, pointless or superficial? Only a well organized, well-integrated mind, with clearly defined and worthwhile contents can be properly educated. Acquiring information, knowledge or skills prior to doing all we can to improve the existing contents of our mind is equivalent to trying to build a beautiful and expensive edifice atop a weak and unsound foundation – the outcome is predictable.

Each of must summon the courage to admit that at least a portion of the contents of our mind is faulty, and must be improved. We must be willing to evaluate the contents of our mind with a determination to discard some things, to reorganize and reclassify others, and to revise and reshape others. We must be willing to make changes in the way we think about some things and feel toward them. We must be willing to admit that some of the subjects we focus our attention on are not the best, and that some of the thoughts we have about things are of inferior quality. We must be willing to admit that our logic is not always the best, and that some of our beliefs, values and principles can be improved as well. We must be willing to do all these things or we will never be able to improve the existing contents of our mind; and, as a result, we will never be able to become properly educated.

THE INTERNALIZATION PROCESS

The previous two sections of this book have dealt with the existing contents of the mind. An area of study entirely different is: that which is yet to become contents of the mind. I have already dealt with that which is yet to become contents in a person's mind in connection with thinking for oneself, but not in connection with the actual incorporation of information or knowledge into a person's mind and life; a process which is commonly called learning, but which I refer to as the *internalization process*. The internalization process refers to making what you are to learn a feeling, acting, breathing and integrated part of you, as opposed to simply memorizing it or only partially learning it.

Being able to recall something when questioned, or in an exam, has been the main criteria for successful learning advanced by educators in this country and around the world. This indicates that education has been widely occurring on a superficial level. Because a person knows something in the sense that he can recall it verbally, or in an exam, is no indication of the quality of its internalization into his mind and life. In fact, knowing something can be a detriment to a person's mind and life.

When it becomes clear that true learning involves the harmonious internalization of something into a person's mind and life, other things also become clear. For instance, it becomes clear that it is not good to know things that are not useful for one to know; or that do not in any way apply to one's needs, desires or inclinations; or that take the place of other things one would be better off learning. It becomes clear that learning is good only to the extent that what is being learned can be personalized for one's own use. Just as excess baggage is a burden to a person, so is excess knowing. As throwing a wrench in working machinery fouls it up, an inappropriate, discordant, or only partially integrated piece of information or knowledge disturbs a person's balance, integrity and identity, and unnecessarily complicates a person's life. (In the process of coming in contact with new things, and in the process of internalizing something, a person's frame of reference may be temporarily upset and he may temporarily feel unbalanced and out of sorts. But this is not a very functional state, and must be repaired before life can resume normally.)

To internalize something is to give it the highest honor. It is as sacred a business as choosing a mate. It is only a small percentage of what a person encounters that he will eventually internalize. That small percentage must be the right things; and the right things can only be the best that are available. To settle for less, or to choose prematurely, would be to do oneself a grave injustice, for that which you internalize into your mind and life is that which you are. Who wants to be second rate – a collection of inferior matter, so that when he looks at himself or thinks of himself, he does so with distaste? If one is not watchful of what he allows to take root in his consciousness, this is what will happen; and this is why the internalization process is so important. It is the internalization process that can improve or corrupt consciousness. We want, then, to perform the internalization process properly.

Inasmuch as the conscious mind has existing contents at the time of confronting any piece of information or knowledge, and cannot act independently of those contents, if a piece of information or knowledge is to be learned; in other words, integrated harmoniously into a person's mind and life; a question that arises – the major question – is how can it be done within the conditions those existing contents must necessarily set forth? Yes, how can it be done? Think of all the effort a person goes through in selecting what beliefs and style of life he has. A person cannot avoid many heartfelt struggles and difficult decisions in becoming the person he is; at least, certainly not in a modern world, where we are all exposed to so many alternatives of behavior and belief. Add to this the fact that each person is complex and peculiar to himself as to his reactions, thought processes, preferences and inclinations; and you must come to the conclusion that integrating something harmoniously into the existing contents of one's mind and life is a complicated and personal process, as is the decision to attempt to do so.

The first thing to be aware of is: things that one is considering for internalization should have been approved of in terms of thinking for oneself. Considering something for internalization, if it follows a rational procedure, occurs after having positive experiences in thinking for oneself about it. In having thought for oneself about something one is considering for internalization, one must have isolated it from the material it was associated as a complete thing, or isolated it and turned it into a complete thing; decided it was a legitimate and worthwhile thing; decided that it applied to him; decided he was currently prepared to relate to it further; and he must have changed its format into the one that best suited him, with positive results. Then he must have established an approach to thinking about it, with positive results. His experience with these things will tell him a lot about whether it is the right thing for him to *attempt* to internalize into the contents of his mind and life. The fact that it was a good thing to think for himself about does not necessarily mean that it is a good thing for him to internalize. Thinking for oneself about something, for example, may be simply of experiential value; and, after the thing has passed through the person's life, leaving some sort of subtle beneficial effect, the person has no more direct contact with it. The criteria for internalizing something – which are *in addition* to the criteria already set forth for thinking for oneself about something, follow in three alternatives:

(1) It must be able to blend into a person's current life and thought processes, producing beneficial results.

(2) Or, it must be able to become a logical extension of a person's current life and thought processes, producing beneficial results.

(3) Or, its internalization must result in an acceptable transformation or radical alteration of a person's current life and thought processes, producing beneficial results.

A person should decide which alternative applies to the thing he is considering for internalization into the contents of his mind and life. If he cannot find validity in any of the three possibilities, internalization of the item is out of the question.

To really convey an understanding of all that is involved in the internalization process, I feel it is best to take a piece of information or knowledge up to, then through, this set of three alternatives. For this purpose, imagine a person who is reading a novel. He comes across the description of a beautiful romance that affects him strongly, but he is unsure why he is so moved by the words. It seems to him that the words might have a special meaning when applied to his own life, but he cannot immediately discern why this is so. He decides to apply the principles set forth in the sections in this book on thinking for oneself and the internalization process. In doing so, the first thing he must determine is why the words affect him so strongly. After he understands what about the words is affecting him so strongly, he will have real information with which to decide what, if any, significance they have when applied to his own life. So he distills the passage, and realizes that the author is trying to point out the "magnificence of true love," and this is what moved him so. Thus, the reader has isolated the thing in its complete form. Now the reader must decide if the thing is true and worthwhile, if it applies to him, if he is prepared to concern himself with such a matter, and in what format he wants it. He thinks about these things, and decides that there *is* such a thing as true love. However, he is responding to a vague, deeply hidden feeling inside himself. He does not know that it is true, but senses that it is. Furthermore, he feels that this truth applies to everyone, himself included. He also feels that it is an important truth, and that he should think about it further, and that there is time and room in his life to occupy himself at times with thoughts about it. Now he must decide if "the magnificence of true love" is the correct format insofar as his mind and life are concerned. He mulls it over, and determines that the "magnificence of true love" is the format in which he wants the matter. He formulates an approach to thinking about "the magnificence of true love" (this may involve such things as how often he will think about it, if he will take notes on the subject or read articles on the subject, and so forth); thinks about it periodically, and decides that he wants to internalize it into his thought processes and life. Now we come to the current place of departure, and are again faced with the three alternatives I posed. Will it *blend into* his current life and thought processes, producing beneficial results? Or can it become a *logical extension* of his current life and thought processes, producing beneficial results? Or can its internalization result in an *acceptable transformation or radical alteration* of his current life and thought processes, producing beneficial results? He thinks about these alternatives. After an interval of considering the alternatives, he begins to realize that the concept will not blend into his current life and thought processes as he has not thought about love in this way for years. The fact is, he long ago forgot about true love; and has been looking only to love, and be loved in return. He also decides that "the magnificence of true love" cannot even be a logical extension of his current life and thought processes because he has for years made a point of dating several women at a time so that he would not be trapped into an emotional dependence upon any one of them. Consequently, if he is to internalize "the magnificence of true love," it must be as an *acceptable transformation or radical*

87

alteration in his current life and thought processes, producing beneficial results. Now, if he internalizes the concept into this thought processes and life, his former view of love is going to have to be sacrificed; and, likewise, his commitments based on his former view of love. He is going to have to change his style of life, insofar as his love life is concerned, so that his love life will more approximately conform to the new addition to his beliefs. He must decide if he is able to do this, and if he really wants to do it. He seriously considers these things, and decides that he can internalize "the magnificence of true love" into the contents of his mind and life by using alternative number three, resulting in beneficial results; and that he wants to do it. He has decided that even though he has enjoyed dating several women at a time, it has caused his life to become too fragmented, and empty of that beautiful feeling of total and unconditional love; and that he is willing to make some temporary sacrifices while in search of the type of love that he had read about in the novel.

For the purpose of internalizing a piece of information or knowledge into the contents of one's mind and life, a few other considerations are appropriate. They have to do with positioning and priorities. For example, a piece of information or knowledge may be placed in the foreground of a person's mind or in the background. It may be placed at the center of his life or merely at the circumference. It may be placed close to certain other information or knowledge, or far away from it. Such spatial comparisons are invaluable when thinking in terms of the existing contents of your mind. Priorities refers to the relative value of things in a person's mind. If the thing is highly valued, it will be given first, or near first, priority of focus. If not so highly valued, it will be given a much lesser priority of focus. (The material in this paragraph is also useful in keeping an account of the contents of one's mind: bookkeeping in the QUALITY OF KNOWING section.)

Since the internalization of an item of information or knowledge, a process which technically begins at the point of thinking for oneself about something, has been shown to involve so many steps and decisions; it should now be apparent that true learning, which is the process of harmoniously internalizing a piece of information or knowledge into the contents of one's mind and life, is no simply matter, and the type of education that has been in vogue in this country, and around the world, is wholly inadequate and often counter-productive.

88

THE REACTION PROCESS

If the internalization process is to have an opportunity to occur without obstacles or impediments, a person's reactions to things must be uncontaminated.

A reaction is involvement unfolding. It is in reacting to things that we fully understand how they affect us. If our reactions are not freely completed, the effects of things upon us are not fully understood. For this reason, people must assume responsibility in completing their own reactions to things; and others must grant them optimum conditions for doing so.

Anything that comes in contact with a person's awareness has the potential of stimulating the person into reacting to it.

A person can react to something in an endless variety of ways: by contemplating it, arguing about it, asking a question about it, reading about it, putting himself in undefined association with it to see what he comes up with, etc. And things that seem to be very removed from the reaction process might well be a part of it. For example, spontaneously going on a boat ride could serve in the contemplating of an idea, and thereby be a part of a person's reaction to the idea.

A reaction can last seconds or years. Sometimes a reaction to something will remain dormant for weeks, months or even years before it renews itself.

Frequently, there is more than one step or phase to a person's reaction to something. And, often, not even the person can see the steps and phases he is going to go through when reacting to something. For example, do you know how you would react if I struck you? I doubt it. It would depend a great deal on what you considered my motive to be, how you responded to me in general and on your current mood. And, even if you knew in advance what all those things would be at the point of my striking you, you may still not know how you would initially react until you actually did so. But reaction, itself, often merely tells you how close you are to the target, giving you food for comparison. What happens to you, and the thing you are reacting to in the process of reacting, plays a substantial part in determining the content of the reaction process.

Externally imposed discipline, rules, guidance and procedures can have a very high danger content because they threaten the reaction process, often preventing important instances of reaction from occurring at all. When reactions are prevented from occurring, it is often the case that the person whose reactions have been prevented from occurring is not even aware of it.

It is due to frequently unexpressed reactions as a result of the circumvention of reactions by persons or circumstances, and as a result of the discouragement of reactions by culture and environment, more so than it is due to inadequacies in native or even learned intelligence, that we have people who mature late or who never mature; and that we have people of little sophistication and awareness.

Let me give you an example of how circumventing reactions prevents people from growing up. Let us say that Johnny is given a host of assignments throughout a school semester that are unappealing to him. His teacher says he must do them and so do his parents. He does them in spite of urges to do other things instead. He may be unaware that the urges he is neglecting for the sake of the assignments he must do are important to be followed, and would eventually lead to the proper unfolding of his personality and identity. If he represses these vital urges enough times, he may lose contact with them, and one day they may not return. This is one of the main ways in which lives are ruined.

Parents and educators should take special note of this, and see to it that the reactions of children and students, in the form of every kind of response, including interest, disinterest, contemplation, rebellion, partial interest, obsessed interest, and bizarre interest, are respected and not infringed upon; and that they are not preempted by the provision of expectations, rules, regulations or procedures invented by others. (This does not apply, of course, if the person is engaging in something immediately and seriously dangerous to his or someone else's well-being, such as reckless automobile driving or the use of hard core drugs.) And all persons who are old enough to think should do their utmost to guard the integrity of their reactions against every form of alternative or substitute behavior.

RESPONSIBILITY FOR ONE'S OWN LEARNING PROCEDURE

The typical student in our schools walks into his classroom or classrooms with the expectation of receiving information he is to absorb, getting assignments and taking tests. This shows he is not responsible for his own learning procedure. At best, he fills in the details of procedure that is outlined for him. This method of education is faulty for the following reasons:

(1) It usurps students' sense of responsibility.

(2) It diminishes students' decision-making opportunities, limits their options and choices, and deprives them of challenges that are rightfully theirs.

(3) It deprives students of their independence, and encourages them to be submissive.

(4) It is disrespectful of each student's self-development, and works to remove him or her from being connected with it.

Many educators and others believe that, as long as students are given some options and choices while engaged in studying and learning, it is adequate to ensure that they are not being overly manipulated or controlled and that their personal needs are being met. This brings to mind many analogies which reveal its absurdity, and I would like to share one with the reader. To assist me in demonstrating my point, I'll ask you, the reader, to accept the proposition that you wish to engage in some sports activity next weekend. A friend of yours, who has the same idea in mind, insists that you play tennis with him. He gives you unlimited options and choices if you will do so. He tells you that you may pick the time, the place, and the duration of the match. You may freely select a racket from his collection, pick the side of the court you wish to play on; and you may elect to keep score or simply hit balls back and forth to one another. You may even take as many rest periods as you wish, in case you are out of shape; and you may elect to serve every ball, or not serve at all. Certainly, in this example, you are given many choices; and, at first glance, it would appear that your friend is being very good to you. However, what if you have no interest in the game of tennis; have found that you have no aptitude for it; have bad ankles that do not lend themselves well to the game of tennis; and, furthermore, you have your heart set on going swimming, a sport you adore and seldom get to do? Would you then be pleased, or comfortable, with all the choices your friend has given you? Of course not. The exact same comparison can be applied to choice of *subject matter and procedure* while learning. The student who is permitted to make choices in connection with his learning activities, but only within the parameters assigned to him by his teachers and by school policy, will most likely not be a happy or prosperous student. He may do what he is told to do, but he will not be getting out of his studies the good that he should. Responsibility for assigning learning goals and for formulating learning procedure must become the prerogative of the student and cease being an automatic right belonging to teachers and administrators.

While I don't believe there is anything inherently wrong with providing *willing* students with learning activities, projects, lessons or assignments – as long as plenty of unencumbered free time is allotted to students for the discovery of their own direction and the pursuit of their own interests; at the points in which students cease being willing participants in, or are resentful of, what educators have devised for them to learn, I believe educators must step back and assess the possible damage they might be inflicting on their students.

By establishing a specific learning curriculum for students, complete with strict rules of participation and performance, teachers and school administrators in this country prevent their students from experiencing much of the joy of learning, and many of its most exciting challenges. By demanding so much from their students, teachers are indirectly asserting that they know what is best for their students concerning their learning needs; but teachers and school administrators seem not to have thought of inquiring about the nature of their students' actual learning needs. If teachers and school administrators were serious about wanting to do a good job of teaching, they would first try to determine what the learning needs of their students are; and the results they arrived at would have to be approved of by their students before they could be seen to have genuine relevance to their needs. One of the facts that such an inquiry would reveal is that students have a need to have <u>final say</u> in *choosing their own subject matter to be learned and formulating their own learning procedure. (Learning procedure* encompasses such things as which books a person will read and which studying aids he will select, what thoughts he will think, which persons he will learn from, what studying techniques he will develop, and which learning goals he will assign himself.)

Several years after I wrote the last paragraph, I discovered that the renowned educator, father of the homeschooling movement and children's rights activist, John Holt, held an identical point of view. In his book, *What Do I Do Monday*, Chapter Fourteen, he said, "Let me sum up what I have been saying about learning. I believe we learn best when we, not others, are deciding what we are going to try to learn, and when, and how, and for what reasons or purposes; when we, not others, are in the end choosing the people, materials, and experiences from which and with which we will be learning; when we, not others, are judging how easily; or quickly or well we are learning, and when we have learned enough ...."

Teachers and school administrators in this country have gotten so bogged down in their limited idea of what education consists of that most of them seem never to have stopped to inquire about the skills that might be needed to sensibly manage and direct the knowledge they are so intent that their students should acquire. Most teachers and school administrators in this country have not squarely faced up to the idea that all knowledge is worthless unless it is possessed by those who have acquired the skills needed to be capable users of that knowledge. It is in this connection that the importance of *choosing one's own subject matter to be learned and formulating one's own learning procedure* becomes evident.

To be a capable user of knowledge, a person must be self-sufficient and self-reliant. He must be able to motivate himself and assume responsibilities. He must have acquired an ability to think for himself, and be able to make sound judgments and intelligent decisions. He must be able to successfully manage his own affairs. And he must be inclined to confront rather than avoid life's most important challenges. This is a pretty tall order, but without acquiring a proficiency at these skills, all else a student learns will be pointless. Without these skills, a student graduate may be stuffed full of information and knowledge, but he will be poorly equipped to use it. (In addition to having the skills I just listed, a person who is to be a responsible, as well as a capable, user of knowledge must be guided by a desire to be a truly good person, and he must be unwilling to plunder or exploit others in order to achieve his own aims. But this is a matter of morals, and is not the focus of this essay.)

So how does a student set himself upon the road to becoming a capable user of knowledge, and how can this objective be furthered by his instructors and by school policy?

To develop the skills needed to become a capable user of knowledge, a student must be provided with the opportunity to *choose his own subject matter to be learned and his own learning procedure.* Being engaged in *choosing one's own subject matter to be learned and one's own learning procedure* on a regular and consistent basis throughout the course of one's learning career, which includes wrestling with all the dilemmas and challenges of doing so, calls upon a student to exercise and perfect the skills needed to become a capable user of knowledge, namely: managing one's own affairs, motivating oneself, thinking for oneself, assuming responsibility, confronting life's challenges, making decisions and judgments of a comprehensive nature, and self-reliance.

I think everyone will agree that an adult who cannot manage his own affairs, motivate himself, think for himself, assume responsibility, confront life's challenges, make decisions and judgments of a comprehensive nature, and rely on himself when his circumstances are difficult or complex, is in a lot of trouble. Likewise, when youngsters are allowed to graduate from schools in a learning program which divests them of their right and their need to apply these skills within all aspects of their learning, they are pointed toward trouble in later years. To become a self-sufficient adult, a youngster must work at being a self-sufficient student. To be able to manage his own affairs as an adult, a youngster must be given the opportunity to manage his own affairs as a student. To be able to think for himself as an adult, a youngster must first attempt to think for himself as a student; which he cannot do unless he is given the opportunity to decide what and how he will learn. To be able to motivate himself as an adult, a youngster must first struggle with motivating himself as a student; which means being given the option of not learning anything so that he will be required to motivate himself to learn something. To be able to confront life's challenges as an autonomous adult, a youngster must be allowed to confront all the challenges of being an autonomous student, with assistance provided by teachers when it is needed or sought.

Submissive and obedient students will likely end up being submissive and obedient adults. Can we realistically expect a different outcome? Teachers and school administrators vastly underestimate the capability of their students, and completely ignore the aspirations of humankind, when they make their students pawns of their educational aims and methods. It is independent-minded youngsters, who are given the opportunity to think for themselves, make their own decisions and manage their own affairs within all aspects of their careers as students, who will most likely end up being capable users of the knowledge they are acquiring.

I know that strong objections to my concept of *choosing one's own subject matter and learning procedure* will come from educators of young children and from educators of young, and older, adults. Educators of young children will say that young children don't have the ability to *choose their own subject matter and learning procedure*; therefore should not be given any responsibility for doing so. Educators of young, and older, adults will say that adults are usually no longer immersed in the process of self-development, and usually take classes to learn specific information in order to advance their careers; and, consequently, have no interest in, nor need for, *choosing their own subject matter and learning procedure*. I can only reply that any facts, information, knowledge, awareness or skills *acquired* while a student (regardless of age) is involved in *subject matter he has selected and learning procedure he has designed* will have been much more happily learned on average, and will be of greater benefit to the student, than the same material learned by means of the techniques of compulsory learning, which prompt a student to do what he is told in order to fulfill the expectations and requirements of teachers and administrators. Just as there is more than one way to cut a cake, there is more than one way to teach the same knowledge, information and skills. Those who use their imagination should be able to figure out ways of teaching both young children and adults that enable them to select their own subject matter to be learned, their own learning materials, their own methods of study and their own studying goals. This method of teaching would require much more input from students and more creativity on the part of the educator; and the role of the teacher would be changed to that of assisting students to find their own path of learning, rather than deciding things for them. Nonetheless, I believe that young children can benefit greatly from being encouraged to make their own choices in all matters connected with the learning process; and that adults of all ages, studying all subjects, at all levels of sophistication, can benefit greatly from designing their own studying goals and studying techniques, according to their own interests and needs. Even if this method of learning is slower, the time spent doing it is much more fulfilling than time spent learning within regimes of enforced education, where choices are few and often begrudgingly granted.

I understand that my concept of learning, which includes choosing one's own learning materials, methods of study and studying goals, will seem like a farcical proposition in the context of studying those subjects which require that exact information be learned and precise procedures or techniques be acquired, such as would be the case in the study of law or medicine. But there are two important reasons why, even when students are studying subjects such as these, their options and choices should be maximized. One of the reasons is that students are not robots; and, as more freedom of choice is introduced into their schoolwork, in connection with what they are to study and how they are to study, students studying even the most precise and demanding subjects will feel more like human beings instead of like robots. The other reason is that to learn anything, that which is to be learned must be personalized to suit one's own mind and life; and the chances that this will occur increase proportionately as a student is permitted to participate more fully in the decision-making process within all aspects of the learning process.

So, how does a student go about *choosing his own subject matter and learning procedure*? Does he call out to the gods, and wait for their reply? And what does he do if they never reply? Remain stupid? Does he look deeply into himself for an area of interest, and pursue it when he finds it? Does he just start out learning, and find his way as he ricochets off his reactions? Well, of course, it is up to him. But what if a student likes the sound of *choosing his own subject matter and learning procedure*; and, upon trying it, finds out that he can't make much headway at it? What if he finds out that every time he tries it, it is not long before he sees a dead end just in front of him? Well, I hope you will not be surprised if I tell you this is probably normal. It is not easy to *choose your own subject matter and learning procedure*. It is much more complex and demanding than blindly following another, as is currently done in education. There are the constant, prodding questions: "Is this the right thing to do? Is this the best thing to do? What if I fail? What if I am wasting my time? What do I want? Why am I doing this?" *Choosing your own subject matter and learning procedure* is, indeed, a battle with your own existence. But less is not learning, never was learning, and never will be learning.

CAN STUDENTS LEARN EFFECTIVELY WHEN THEIR LEARNING IS NOT MANDATORY?

Public education in this country currently operates on the premise that learning must, in large part, be mandatory if it is to be successful. From the very beginning, young students are made to feel the pressure of *required learning*. True, the learning that youngsters do is often interspersed with fun activities, and teachers attempt to make learning enjoyable and agreeable to their students; nonetheless, a significant portion of the learning that youngsters do is *required* of them; and, if they do not do it, they are reprimanded or punished. Many of the private schools instruct in the same manner; and, many of the private schools that claim to offer a more relaxed learning environment, in which students may be more selective in choosing what and how they will study, still impose some learning requirements upon their students. Educating without imposing mandatory learning requirements of any kind is rare within schools; but I believe it is a viable, healthy and dynamic approach to educating students of all ages. I think it is a particularly useful approach to educating our youngsters; and that, for that purpose, it is the best avenue possible. Many homeschoolers already successfully use this approach, and have much to teach professional educators about its philosophy and techniques.

I believe that teaching without mandatory learning require-ments of any kind is particularly beneficial to youngsters *because* all young people are in the process of a sensitive search for all aspects of their own identities, and are busy making the difficult choices that will ultimately determine the kind of people they will become. If the things youngsters are to learn, and the overall direction of their learning, are determined by others, such as by teachers and by school policy, it can encroach upon or disrupt the natural process of development and the actual learning needs of the youngsters; and, when that happens, the learning process becomes harmful and destructive. Reading specific books, focusing on specific subject matter, or adhering to specific studying methods or goals concocted by a specific teacher or by the policy of a specific school, does not guarantee that anything good will be accomplished; but, it does suggest the creation of problems for young students. In the first place, arbitrarily invented studying goals vary widely, and cannot be said to be equally worthwhile. But, of much greater significance is the extent to which studying goals, techniques and subject matter coincide with the learning needs of students.

Since each young student is a unique individual, with different habits, needs, moods, attitudes, inclinations, abilities, capacities and growth patterns, and since the circumstances of each young student's life may vary greatly, each young student has different learning needs. Teaching that is going to be effective and constructive must coincide with the learning needs of each student. Proper teaching must be individually tailored in terms of content and methods of instruction. Often it is only subtle variations in studying content and methods of instruction that will make all the difference. For example, a young student may be indifferent to carpentry; but when it is suggested that he try to build a particular thing he has always wanted, his interest perks.

There are many ways of instructing students which are very effective, but impose no mandatory studying requirements; yet, which still require effective teaching skills. In a classroom or school in which there are *no* mandatory studying requirements, a teacher can encourage, challenge, inspire, stimulate, help and guide her students; and she can provide them with unlimited learning aids, and with endless resources from which to learn.

If a teacher has a lot to offer her students, and has earned her students' respect because of her qualities as a person, and because of her abilities to relate to students on a very basic and human level, the students will be receptive to what she has to offer; and, more so if it is being offered without pressure or force.

All youngsters want to improve their lives, develop their talents, and wish to occupy their time in some useful way; or, will eventually be made aware of the good sense of these objectives as they gain a little in life-experience and maturity. A teacher who is skilled at tapping into these sensible and natural impulses can teach just as surely, I believe, as a teacher using the old methods of required or compulsory learning; and, can teach much more constructively because she will be teaching in harmony with the actual needs and natural impulses of the students.

I would like now to describe some of the characteristics of the type of school I envision; that is, one which operates entirely on the premise of teaching without the use of *any* mandatory studying requirements.

The teachers who teach in such a school must be hand-picked for their ability to teach within its educational framework. When initially interviewed for a teaching position at the school, they would be asked how they felt about teaching in a school in which there are *no* mandatory studying requirements, except the very general requirement that the students be able to benefit from being there and participating in its programs. The prospective teachers would also be asked what they felt they had to contribute to such a school, and how they would go about teaching in such a school. The teachers would be selected for their expertise in useful knowledge, their maturity, their knowledge of life and how to live life successfully, their ability to gain the trust and camaraderie of the students; and their ability to encourage, inspire and guide the students in the learning process.

The classes offered in the school could be of any length, and in any subject the teacher deems useful to the students, so long as some students became willing participants in them. The students would be given a daily schedule of the ongoing classes and the planned or impromptu educational events; and could wander into and out of them at will.

Those teachers who could stimulate and encourage students to participate in voluntary learning activities without badgering them, harassing them or threatening them; and who could accommodate their students' requests to learn those subjects and skills that appealed to them (the students); and who could teach in a manner that corresponds to the learning needs and learning inclinations of their students – would be the successful teachers in such a school.

The students in this school would be encouraged to engage in independent learning activities of all kinds; and they would be encouraged to freely make requests of the teachers for learning tools and resources, and for instruction tailored to suit their learning needs and learning inclinations, regardless of how different or unusual those may be.

Within this school would be all sorts of learning opportunities that are valuable to the students' present lives and for preparing them for adulthood. Many practical trades and skills would be offered by expert craftsmen and artisans. Nor would science, literature or the arts be neglected. An active social life for the students would be encouraged, and much attention would be paid to the proper development of each youngster's character. Work-for-money programs would be found in plenty at the school, or would be arranged by working in tandem with outside industry, so the youngsters could learn the discipline of hard work and the skills of getting along in the workplace. Volunteer work that is humanitarian in nature would be promoted and encouraged at the school so that students could learn the virtue and benefits of giving from the earliest age, and so that acts of charity could be inculcated into their concept of how life should be lived.

Some students would adapt well to learning in such a school. Those who do not adapt well to learning particular subjects or skills within such a learning environment may, nonetheless, benefit from the experience of simply being in it; and, if they do, should be permitted to remain. Those students who benefit little from such an environment, or interfere with the learning opportunities of other students, would be suspended or expelled. Teachers who appear at first to have the qualities for being good instructors in such an environment, but ultimately fail at being able to teach successfully within it, would have their jobs at the school terminated.

A school such as the one just described would be a school designed to facilitate self-directed learning. If the end goal of education is to produce self-sufficient, self-directed, capable people, doesn't it seem plausible that the educational process, itself, can be more enriching and produce better results if learning is accomplished by means of self-initiated, self-directed and self-regulated studies? And if the end goal of education is to produce self-sufficient, self-directed, capable individuals, isn't it a bit suspicious when the bulk of a student's formal learning occurs as a result of expectations and requirements imposed upon him by others?

If a student can learn by means of self-directed learning, made possible and assisted by the appropriate teachers, and a school policy which endorses and promotes it; we can be sure that his learning relates to and pertains to him, and to his own needs and growth patterns; and we can be sure that the manner of his learning will be appropriate for him and comfortable. But when learning is done by demand, we are never sure if it corresponds to a student's needs, abilities or interests; or if it is harmonious with his particular psychology or growth patterns; and consequently we risk endangering the identity, the psyche, and the happiness and peace of mind of the student.

In a school designed for the purpose self-directed learning, the school grounds and buildings might appear similar to any other school; but the curriculum available for study, the teaching methods of the teachers and learning habits of the students would not resemble their counterparts in a traditional public school, or in most private schools. The differences in his schooling, from a youngster's point of view, would begin with his *choices of subject matter, methods of study and studying goals*. Instead of being restricted or limited in number, choice of subject matter would be limited only by the interests of the student; and choices of methods of study and studying goals would be confined only to the limits of the student's imagination and needs.

I feel it would be helpful to walk a student through a typical day in such a school in order to show, in greater detail, how such a school might operate. Since every student has a name and an age, I shall name our imaginary student Ralph, who is ten years of age.

It is now Ralph's first day at this unusual school, which is founded upon the principles of self-directed learning. Ralph is about to be given a verbal introduction to the school and a walk-through orientation. His introduction and orientation may be conducted by a teacher, by one of his peers, or by one of the older students in the school who has become well-versed in the ways of the school. Ralph is told that, in this school, entirely different things will be expected of him than are normally expected of youngsters in a public or private school setting. He is told that he will be expected to find a path of being and learning within the school which he is comfortable with, and which can benefit him in the present as well as contribute to his future needs as an adult. He is told that while attending the school, he will be expected to learn, progress and enjoy himself; but the avenues or means by which he accomplishes that within the school will be his choice entirely. He is told that the teachers are available to assist and help him, but are never permitted to force or pressure him to study. He is told that behavior of his which disrupts the work of the teachers, or interferes with the learning activities of the other students in the school, is unacceptable; and is cause for suspension or expulsion from the school.

While on this tour, Ralph is introduced to various teachers and students, and made to feel at home in the environment. He is treated with respect and dignity; and as if he is someone special, and capable of fine accomplishments. He is taken to many different ongoing classes or programs of useful instruction so that he can see how they operate, with the hope that one or more of the classes or programs will arouse his interest. If it appears that one has sparked his interest, the tour guide will dally there a bit and give Ralph a chance to investigate further.

It is pointed out to Ralph that in this school, while there are paid staff who are all experts in their field, everyone in the school is encouraged to teach and learn from one another; which means that the students are free to engage in instructing and helping one another; and, in like fashion, the teachers may instruct and help one another; and the students may instruct and help the teachers, when that possibility arises. In this school, all who participate are considered students and teachers at various stages of evolving; and those who learn and those who teach are not segregated into separate groups, but are blended together into a purposeful mix of getting the most out of the school environment.

In taking Ralph to the area in which instruction in carpentry occurs, a note of curiosity and enthusiasm appears on his face. Here can be found boys and girls building various projects of interest to them, with instructors roaming freely among them and making themselves available for assistance. The students are of various ages, and at various stages of building their different items. One student is building a chair, another a coffee table, another a bookshelf, while several of the younger students are busy building wooden toys. Some of the students are going over books on carpentry, while a couple of the students who are complete novices are busy practicing pounding nails into wood and sawing lengths of wood. Books on carpentry instruction line the walls; and some tools of the trade that are in view are lying idle, ready for use.

An attempt is made by the tour guide to introduce Ralph to the instructors present and as many of the students as possible, so that he can feel at home in the class. The students and teachers create an atmosphere of acceptance for Ralph, and encourage him to return to the carpentry class and get involved. One of the instructors asks Ralph a few questions about his interest in carpentry and experience, to see if he might suggest a project for him that he might be interested in building, and that is within the scope of his present carpentry skills.

Moving on from the carpentry area, Ralph is given a

complete tour of the grounds and facilities, and is permitted to ask any questions concerning the school or his upcoming participation within it. All rules and regulations of the school are fully explained to him, and support literature is provided. A general history of the school is given to him, as well as its general economic status. An effort is made to introduce Ralph briefly to the school administrators so that he can have a more complete picture of the school, and so that he can realize that the entire school tries to operate as if its members are one large family.

Finally, Ralph is told that he will be given adequate time to adjust to the ways of the school, and to find a niche for himself within it. He is told that since he is not being pressured or forced to participate in any particular curriculum, he must rely upon his own interests and inclinations to direct him. He is told that since many of us are not used to looking to our inner selves for direction in our education, it is something that takes getting used to. He is told that no one in the school will criticize him if he is slow in finding his true interests and inclinations; and that, as long as he is making an effort to do so, his time in the school will be considered well spent.

HOW TO MOTIVATE ONESELF TO LEARN

Motivating oneself is an important part of being successful at choosing one's own subject matter and learning procedure. In response to the question, "How do I motivate myself to learn?" let me first say that motivating oneself seems to involve either sustaining something, moving (or progressing) toward something, or moving (or progressing) away from something. Without the concepts of sustaining something; moving (or progressing) toward something; or moving (or progressing) away from something, self-motivation appears an impossibility. In the case of learning, self-motivation becomes applicable in the progressing-toward sense of the word. Now that this is clarified, I offer a comparison, and an example, for the purpose of showing how a person can go about motivating himself to learn; in other words, how he can progress toward something in his learning.

First, the comparison. .... If I wish to move a cup from one place to another, there must be a place to which I can move it, and I must do something to it to get it there. In motivating oneself to learn, the same type of situation is present as in getting a cup from one place to another. The same two elements are involved: the objective; that is, the place to get to; and the catalyst, that is, the something that you do to yourself to get you there.

So if you wish to motivate yourself to learn, you must have a place to progress toward in your learning. Then you must do something to yourself to get your there. You must give yourself a push or a pull. This push or pull could be the reward of getting there, the realization of the necessity to get there, inspiring oneself to get there, or whatever. But there must be some continual fuel with which you can get yourself there. (The desire to learn is not a sufficient criterion in motivating oneself to learn, as it implies no specific place to get to. While the desire to learn might be the fuel; that is, the something you do to yourself to get yourself to progress in your learning, it is insufficient without the realization of the place you want to get to in your learning.)

We are still lacking a practical example. Let me bring myself into this example, and propose that I want to study history. If I am going to make any real headway, I must decide upon a place I want to get to in the learning of history. I also must have a catalyst I shall use to get myself there. That catalyst will be as an apple held in front of a horse to lead him somewhere. In other words, it will serve as an impetus or a go-between. It is that which enables the transition to occur between where one is and where one is going. It is the link, as it were, the bridge, the road along which one will travel. And, strangely enough, that bridge, or however it is thought of, may not necessarily be related to either the place where one is or the place to which one is going. It might just be a stimulant. Now, to continue with my example. .... Upon dabbling into the subject of history, I discover in myself an interest in a certain historian. Realizing I must have an objective if I am to make any real headway in the study of history, I look for that objective in connection with said historian. I manage to ascertain in myself a sincere desire to read the main body of his work. Thus, one half of the problem is settled. Now I must find a way of motivating myself to do it. I work at it, but cannot seem to get myself going with any degree of intensity. I again examine the objective, and it still satisfies me. The fault, then, lies with the catalyst. In desperation, I remember that I have a very rich uncle, an interesting fact in that I have need of additional money. This uncle likes me a lot, has always been accommodating, and is rather bizarre and unconventional in his outlook on life. I feel that he would appreciate an unusual proposition if it were for a good cause. So I go to that uncle and ask him to offer me a thousand dollars if I finish reading the major body of the historian's work, and I specify that I am not to receive a penny of the money until I have completed the task in its entirety; and I even provide my uncle with a checklist of those books which are considered to be the main body of the historian's work. If my uncle were to accept my proposition, and offer me the thousand dollars on the condition that I read every book on the checklist I provided him; his offer could be just the added incentive, the stimulant, that I need to read the historian's work.

In trying to formulate the places you will go in your learning, and the catalysts you will use to get yourself there, it is crucial to try to pursue and follow your own reactions to that with which you are confronted in your learning activities; as it is these reactions that will reveal the nature of the place, or places, to which it is wise for you to go in your learning, and the type, or types, of catalysts that are needed to get you there. To do this, it is of course necessary to play into your reactions within the learning process, to let them be the focus of your concentration and the pulse of your activity, to become familiar with their language and cues and to take direction from them. Just as driving a car has its own language and cues, a person's reactions within the learning process will have their own language and cues. As you begin to learn to move, and work, with your reactions within the learning process, sensible objectives and their necessary catalysts in your learning will not be difficult to ascertain. That which you could not see with a telescope, you will be able to see with a microscope. That which you could not know of as a stranger, you will be able to know as a friend. That which you bypass ordinarily will show itself to be a world replete with assistance. By paying close attention to your reactions, you are paying close attention to your instincts. It is, perhaps, the greatest form of self-indulgence; but, at the same time, it is the most useful form of it, as it is the basis of all integrity in thought and deed. In becoming absorbed in the subtleties of your reactions as they relate to your learning, uncertainty about your learning goals and motivation becomes less a possibility as it becomes your specialty. To the extent that this uncertainty poses you a real threat, you should become absorbed in the subtleties of your reactions within the learning process. It is an extremely common error to assume that to know more about a subject or area of study is to know more about your direction in it. The truth of the matter is that to know more about your reactions to a subject or area of study is to know more about your direction in relation to it.

THE APPLICATIONS OF KNOWLEDGE

Since knowledge is only as valuable as it is useful; but, more precisely, as it is useful to the person who has it, it follows that a person should not seek a line of progress in his learning that does not conform to his use for what he is learning. A student's learning activities can be no more inspiring to him than are the prospects for making use of what he is studying; and, the more worthwhile application he can find for something, the more meaningful it becomes to him. A student who is aware of this will realize that, in truth, it is not what he knows that is important to him; rather, it is his skill at applying it, and the quality of gain that can thereby be obtained. He will realize that it is infinitely better to have one idea with a few good possible applications in mind for it than to merely have one hundred ideas. He will continually focus on the application of what he knows and is confronted with in his learning activities, and will give it a preference greatly in excess of the acquiring of ideas, facts and information to keep the scales balanced in its favor. He will, in truth, not be a seeker of knowledge. He will be a seeker of the applications of knowledge. If he submits himself to a challenge of what he knows, it will not be for the purpose of testing the quantity of facts and information he possesses. Instead, it will be to determine his skill at applying what he knows. In other words, his will be a "doing" existence. He will learn to despise dormant knowledge, realizing that an inactive piece of knowledge is a useless one which should be replaced by one that can be put to use. By not allowing the lack of use to enter into his acceptance, he maintains his respect for use itself. In seeking to learn the applications of knowledge, and in trying to find opportunities for applying it, a student points himself toward true success in *choosing his own subject matter and learning procedure.* While postponed gain, as advocated by those who believe in acquiring a large body of dormant knowledge and waiting until you graduate to use it, may appear to be theoretically feasible; it is not emotionally healthy. It can be compared to wooing a girl for years before you are allowed to touch her. It is far better to be learning less and applying more of it; than to be learning more, and applying less of it.

107

SPEAKING OUT

A very important aspect of *choosing one's own subject matter and learning procedure* is speaking out. It is a unique fact that our thoughts and feelings often exist at an unconscious level. One of the finest ways of bringing them to the surface so we can view them and understand them is by simply talking about them. One of the finest ways of finding out one's position on a matter is in voicing one's opinions and discussing them. If one's position on a matter is unclear, relating to it must be clumsy and faulty; and so, there is little sense in proceeding in relation to it. In the process of learning, where understanding is critical and the need for it is almost constant, speaking out becomes a prime tool of analysis and clarification. It is essential that teachers and schools make every effort to promote speaking out throughout every facet of the educational process. Those students who are sincerely and enthusiastically engaged in discussion or debate should be praised in this connection, encouraged to continue and not distracted for any reason; and those who avoid speaking out must be encouraged to see what they are missing. And students themselves must look to speaking out as a valuable tool to aid them in *choosing their own subject matter and learning procedure* with wisdom and foresight.

INTROSPECTION AND REFLECTION

Introspection and reflection are other important learning tools. They are strictly contemplative exercises, as opposed to interactive or participative ones in the world at large. Their use is internal adjustment. Continual exposure to things requires continual reorientation; and what better place to conduct that reorientation than behind closed doors, where a person is not subject to the expectations and needs of others, or to the changing currents of circumstance? It is a person's opportunity to drop the social self, the defensive self, even the compassionate self, and see himself when he is not being pulled or distracted by one persuasive influence or another. It is an opportunity to see oneself as a still target, rather than a moving one.

Introspection and reflection are put to use to improve our relationship with things in our mind; that is, to sharpen our focus on them, to organize them better, or to expand our understanding of them by thinking about them from different angles; and they are also used to better evaluate the effects of things upon us. Introspection and reflection contribute significantly to the quality of our mind, and to our ability to deal with what we confront in our daily lives. They are essential tools for keeping the mind in good condition so that proper learning can occur. It is clear that introspection and reflection should be given a high priority if a student is to be successful in *choosing his own subject matter and learning procedure.*

FOUR REASONS WHY LEARNING CAN BE DIFFICULT

It is usually assumed that when a student finds learning difficult, the fault lies in the student's ability to comprehend. While this may be so, there are four other possibilities that need to be examined. An awareness of these will increase the learning know-how of the person who wishes to be a good student; and can help to clarify the teaching process for those educators who are interested in improving their understanding of it. The four other possibilities are: the quality of the subject matter that is presented by educators; the quality of the presentation of that subject matter; the student's preparedness; and the student's approach. I shall discuss them in the order just given.

Subject matter can come to us in all degrees of quality. A student should not be expected to learn subject matter of poor quality without difficulty; when, in fact, even the brightest student may have difficulty learning it, and he would be worse off for it! What is important here is the precise degree to which subject matter warrants being learned. If no such specification is made in connection with the subject matter offered by teachers and schools, one can assume they consider the quality of the subject matter they offer to be beyond reproach. While the subject matter they offer might be very good, it is very unfair to expect students to accept it as good prior to satisfying their judgment that it is. And if students do not, on their own initiative, question the quality of the subject matter offered by teachers and schools, it is the responsibility of educators to see that they do, as it is a sound and necessary aspect of learning procedure. Questioning the merit of a particular author or book, or even the value of an entire area of study, should not be out of bounds in the normal course of learning. In fact just as much, or more, is learned from disagreeing with an author, or opposing a point of view, as is learned by accepting the subject matter one is studying without dissent of any kind. The fact that the question of quality of subject matter seldom arises in a typical classroom as a topic for serious discussion; but is, at best, voiced in a class by a lone wolf who is usually politely disregarded by the teacher and his fellow classmates, shows that something is urgently amiss. That is the tell-tale heart. Where a plausible criticism is never broached, nor regarded as a worthwhile challenge, corruption lies in hiding. Now, if teachers and schools openly stated their impression of the quality of the subject matter they are presenting, and backed up their statements with meaningful defense, defense other than a mere bibliographic cop-out – so and so recommends this and so does so and so, defense that consisted perhaps of what they had gained from the subject matter, or what they see its implications to be; one could at least have some idea of the criteria the teacher or school has for presenting the books, authors, ideas and programs that they do, rather than some other. But if no such defense is voiced, it is logical to assume that the teachers and schools do not want the quality of the subject matter they are offering to be questioned by their students. This is very unfortunate because it would generate healthy debate which, while it may interrupt lesson plans and interfere with pat formulas for teaching, invigorates the learning environment like nothing else can. Students, and teachers who want their students to learn for the right reasons and in ways that are truly beneficial to them, should always examine subject matter of every kind for its quality; and students should be willing to subject it to every critical test before submerging themselves in acquiring it or studying it. And they should realize that inability to learn could well be the fault of subject matter of poor quality.

As subject matter may come in all degrees of quality, so can its presentation. Students who have difficulty learning something have every right to question its presentation. Just as attractively presented, good tasting food will encourage us to devour it, well presented subject matter will encourage us to learn it. And as an unattractive, terrible tasting plate of food (though it has superb nutritional value) will discourage us from eating it, poorly presented subject matter will discourage us from learning it. If it is a really nice looking shoe, a person is going to want to buy a pair if he can spare the money, and then he will hope that his size is available; whereas, though it is a really good shoe and just his size, if it has a dismal appearance, you could not get the same person to touch it. It is the same with learning. Esthetics is important. Educators and students should not discount improper presentation of subject matter as the cause of faulty learning prior to establishing sufficient reason why this could not be so.

Preparedness is a factor that is not given proper respect in the learning environment; perhaps because teachers are impatient to get on with the task at hand, and do not want to have to cope with too many complex challenges. But it must be stressed that a student who is not prepared to learn something cannot be said to lack ability to learn. He cannot even be said to have less intelligence than others. First of all, though he may not be prepared to learn certain subject matter, he may be prepared to learn other subject matter of equal value. This would be simply a matter of suitability of subject matter. Secondly, learning is actually a sub-function. By that, I mean life cannot be measured in its terms. It must be measured in terms of life. Learning is only good insofar as it applies to living and is useful for living. If a student is not prepared to learn certain material as there is not room in his life for it, or it really does not relate to his interests, or other things concern him more – such as making better use of what he already knows, it is not the time for him to learn it. He is not prepared to learn it. At another time, he may be. This has nothing to do with his ability to learn or comprehend. It is, again, merely a matter of suitability. Teachers and schools must always consider these factors a possibility in judging a student's unwillingness or failure to learn. And individuals wishing to be good students should keep preparedness in mind as a crucial factor affecting their learning skills.

The student's approach to what he is learning is another key factor affecting his learning skills. The connection between a student and subject matter to be learned does not occur automatically; rather, it is subject to the student's approach. Someone else's approach cannot be substituted for the student's approach. If you are to pick up a glass, you must have an approach. If you are to drive a car, you must have an approach. If a man is to kiss a woman, he must have an approach. We forget that walking requires an approach; but, before we were able to walk, we were quite aware of the need for an approach to walk. Anything you are to do requires an approach. If you fail to be able to do something, it does not mean that you are unable to do it. It may merely mean that your approach is inadequate. A student who is poor at learning, or at learning some particular thing, may not have stumbled onto the right approach. Do not be quick to condemn him for his clumsiness or ineptness, as underneath may lie great aptitude which merely requires the right approach; which, should he discover it, will make his critics look like ignoble fools, and cause them to question themselves with an intensity equal to their criticism of him. Harken to this fact, all you educators, and students also. The proper approach may be all that is lacking to begin a brilliant learning career.

There are countless different approaches to most everything we might learn or do, many of which we will never discover. This should be remembered; and, if it is, discouragement with trying to learn something we are interested in learning will not precede a large amount of experimentation with approach.

I have next an example of a number of choices of approach to learning the same subject matter, and I show how result varies with approach. The object of our attention is a student studying a given set of historical material. If he studies it with no particular approach, he should not be surprised to arrive at no particular outcome. If his approach is primarily an esthetic one, he would visualize the material and obtain information from it in terms of its entertainment value, its cultural value, and so on. If his approach is primarily a philosophical one, he would visualize the information and obtain data from it in terms of the profound truths inherent in it. If his approach is to understand his own society by picking up facts about such matters as the development of governments and economies, this is what he will gain from his studies of history. If his approach is just for laughs, he may well end up contributing to a career as a budding comedian through his studies of history. As his approach varies, so does the result.

Many people who are poor students, or who are not eager learners, are missing out on a lot of the best that life has to offer. I am not suggesting that anyone should learn just because they are told to; but that all people should find something they really want to learn, and keep working at learning it until they stumble upon the right approach for them. It is usually not the result of being a poor learner, nor an uninterested student, that a person is unable to learn. It is more likely caused by one or more of the four reasons for poor learning I have just presented.

UNLEARNING AND REEVALUATING

Without unlearning, learning could not take place. Unlearning is the art of finding, rooting out and disposing of those things one has absorbed, learned, or is inclined to be that are found to be inappropriate to one's thoughts, feelings, circumstances or lifestyle; or that are found to be surpassed in quality by things which may replace them.

Learning and unlearning can be compared to the doing and undoing of things. If a person ties a knot and decides to untie it; it is likely to be more difficult than tying it, as we all know. If a man flies from America to Japan and decides he wishes he hadn't; to undo it, he has to fly back. If a person throws something away and decides he wants it back, he is likely going to take more time and expend more effort in retrieving it than in discarding it. Unlearning is just the other side of learning, as undoing is the other side of doing. But, for some reason, we never think about that side of the education coin. Yet, if a person is going to learn to be kind, he may have to unlearn the reasons for his cruelty; and if a person is going to learn to read enriching books, he may have to unlearn his habit of reading pornography, etc.

As often as not, the learning of something is dependent upon the unlearning of something else, just because both memory and the ability for involvement are limited.

Sometimes the need for unlearning arises in the form of an emotional obstacle toward learning, such as just not feeling like learning. If this happens, the negative feeling would have to be unlearned if learning is to take place.

If a person feels like learning, but his support for some of the aspects of his current habits or lifestyle will not permit him to, or interfere; he has to unlearn giving them his support if learning is to occur, or if it is to occur as he would like it to.

If a person wishes to learn a particular thing that replaces or contradicts something else in his mind or life, his support for the old will have to be unlearned if sane learning is to take place.

In learning a skill, or undertaking learning which requires a skill to be able to do it, old habits of mind may have to be unlearned. For example, if a hard-core businessman, seldom given to expressing his feelings, wanted to become an artist, he might first have to unlearn some of the habits of mind of an

114

inveterate businessman.

It is a common belief that things that are learned are done so by the mind only; and that, if the mind chooses to forget them, it simply tells them to go away, or casually drops them in the nearest junk pile or wastebasket. But that which has been truly learned, either in an academic sense, or by absorption, or by habit, is a part of a person. It is not in his mind only. To propose that it is makes a mockery of learning. He breathes it, feels it, thinks it, talks it, sees it and hears it. When he wakes up in the morning, he sometimes finds it greeting him hello. When he reads the paper, it may float across the page. When he is sipping his afternoon tea, it should not surprise him to find it staring up at him from the bottom of the cup. When he looks up at the sky, he might see it superimposed on a cloud. He can discard it no more easily than he can discard a part of himself. In unlearning, then, one must alter oneself in some way.

So as not to underestimate the difficulty of unlearning, a person should keep in mind that what he is includes not only what he has learned through absorption and academic learning, but also what he feels and what he does; and he should realize that all these things are intertwined. Let us look at a criminal, for example. A criminal thinks and feels like a criminal. When he looks at a woman, he is more likely to see her pocketbook than his heart. When he walks along the road, he may well be contemplating some aspect of his next "job." When he hears a tune on the radio that is peaceful, he may think of the happiness he can gain from stolen dollars. And a carpenter. .... A carpenter thinks and feels like a carpenter. The rhythms of his pounding stay with him into the night. When he looks at his surroundings, he has a good eye for wooden structures. When a conversation takes a bent toward his trade, his interest perks. But there is more. .... A man who screams often at his wife screams often in his mind. A boy who frequently takes his dog on lazy walks often goes on lazy walks in his mind. A person who has a lot of fun sees the pleasant side of things. A person who is very often sad sees the dark side of things. A person who feels lonely walks along deserted roads in his mind. A person who feels self-pity puts a cage around himself in his mind, and refuses to offer himself the slightest crumb of mercy.

Upon realizing that we really are what we have learned, what we do and what we feel, and that they are all intertwined, a person can begin to look at unlearning with sober intentions and expectations. He will not feel that what he knows, what he does, what he thinks or what he feels can be unlearned without incurring consequences to his daily activities. He will not think that he can unlearn something without finding some type of replacement for the space in his life that it filled, even if that replacement is the willingness to do nothing. He will not think he can unlearn something if there are things in his life very dependent upon it for their support without exerting great effort.

All the things that we think, feel and do are things that we get to know and understand; so that, after awhile, they become old friends of ours. We learn their idiosyncrasies, their needs. We work hard at finding outlets and avenues for them, and at discovering ways of pacifying them and cooperating with them. When there is a better way of thinking, doing or feeling that crosses a person's path and teases the person's interest, the old way will become jealous and flaunt its appeal. It will say, "I am the old way, the proven way. You must have faith in me. Give me time to show you what I can do, and you will not be sorry. Can you think you see all my possibilities when looking through the window of your negative attitude toward me? When was it that I disappointed you? Tell me, and we shall discuss it. Don't you remember the times I helped you? When you had nothing to do, you often called upon me; and I always made myself available to you. Often you sang praises of me. When you let me lapse into the rear of your life, you found yourself shocked at how lost you were without me. If you think you do not need me at this moment, it is because the time is not now that you need me; but that time is coming soon." And when a person begins to acquire a new interest in something, so that his attention is being drawn away from his usual activities, one of his usual activities will say to him in disgust, "Why have you discarded your head pillow and replaced it with a foot pillow? My dear man, you do not think with your feet! Protect your head, not your feet. You have lain your head on me so long, you think that I am part of your head; and that is why you think you can abandon your previous usage of me. But if you look more closely at the facts, you would not dare to do so. And that which you are aspiring to blend into your life at this time shows no promise of worth. It is but a good act by a good actor." Or the usual activities will transform themselves into lonely, unclothed children in the winter snow, and beg him for mercy. They will make him feel ashamed of his neglect. Or the usual activities will transform themselves into protagonists, and hurl at him stark new challenges to entice him back. Or they will bargain with him as the most clever of businessmen, offering great yields at half the usual investment, and new sources of borrowing at low interest. And they will act in unison, showing the needs of each of the usual activities to be the fortress and inspiration of the others. So a person should approach unlearning heavily armed. He should count on struggle, rather than hope there will be none.

That which indicates to what extent learning or unlearning is in order is reevaluation.

A healthy person has a continually shifting consciousness, which perpetually combines learning, unlearning and reevaluating in everything it does. It is constantly examining the way one looks at things and associates with them: reevaluating; it is constantly active at increasing the basic foundation of one's intellect: learning; and it is constantly looking for reasons for, and upon finding them, practicing disassociation: unlearning. The pliability of such a mind is its greatest asset, enabling one not to resort to a static approach to life.

When this type of equality is given to learning, unlearning and reevaluating, things are seen bathed in the light of their alternatives and potential, and life has got to be much more alive than otherwise. It is only those who, once they have learned things, do not unlearn, reevaluate and continue learning who find themselves in mental ruts.

We really cannot expect to stumble onto the right way of doing something the first time, or the proper understanding of a thing in our first conceptual image of it. And it stands to reason that the longer we work at a thing, the better we will become at it; and the longer we conceptualize something, the closer we will get to its true essence. These are good reasons to place great emphasis on the value of unlearning and reevaluating, good reasons to give them a status in education equivalent to that of learning. And if we are ever to change an old way of doing things, or an old thought or deleterious mood that has been ingrained by habit, it is precisely these: unlearning and reevaluating, that we must look to for assistance. This is yet further reason to give them a status in education equivalent to that of learning.

It would be a great comfort to me if, when I asked a person what he was doing with himself, he were to tell me that he was busy unlearning, or reevaluating his actions, thoughts or feelings about things. The would show me that he did not have a prejudice toward learning, which is truly only one side of a two-sided issue: reevaluating being the mediator.

If these three concepts were to become a part of the culture of society, I would run into many people who are unlearning, or who are reevaluating their actions, thoughts and feelings about things. Perhaps some would be unlearning some things, reevaluating others and learning still others at the same time. This would be music to my ears because I would feel that a truly meaningful approach to education had a foothold.

MORE ABOUT UNLEARNING

Unlearning is called for whenever learning has occurred incorrectly, or whenever the wrong things have been learned. A mind that has been force-fed knowledge and information over a period of years; or that has been expected to learn large amounts of information and knowledge hastily, or under conditions which do not favor proper assimilation; or that has been taught many things it need not know or has no use for knowing; or that has been taught by means of teaching methods which were abrasive or uncomfortable .... has been improperly educated, and will have acquired certain ailments and deficiencies as a result.

One of the negative results of improper or unnecessary learning is a cluttered mind. When a person's mind is cluttered with much that is unnecessary or unneeded, those things interfere with clear thinking. It is better that the mind not be introduced to knowledge and information too hastily, or in too great quantity for it to properly assimilate it or thoroughly react to it. A mind that learns slowly and sparingly has a better opportunity to evaluate and integrate what it is learning, and can more readily enjoy the learning process. A mind that is force-fed information and knowledge, or that is expected to hastily memorize or review large amounts of information and knowledge, cannot properly evaluate or assimilate it; and will probably not enjoy the learning process, or will not enjoy it in the way that it should.

So, what is the cure for all this bad and improper learning? I suggest the creation of one or more classes in unlearning on every school campus. One of the tasks of a class in unlearning would be to spot those deficiencies and ailments that have been created in a person by too much learning, by unnecessary learning, by improper methods of learning, or by exposure to inadequate or improper methods of teaching. Another of the tasks of such a class would be that of mapping out the contents of one's mind so that one can get a clear idea of all that is in there and why it was put there in the first place; to see if it should be allowed to remain, or if it should be revised. Another of the tasks of such a class would be to plan a strategy for ridding the mind of all that is in it that should not be there. In a class dedicated to unlearning, students could also try to discover if their current learning is occurring properly; and if the things they are learning are needed or desired by them; and if the teaching methods used by their teachers are suitable to their learning needs. In such a class, speculation and debate about ways of uncluttering the mind, and better identifying, organizing and revising its contents would be commonplace. A listing of the types of things each student does not want to learn or would like to unlearn can be attempted. Different ways of unlearning might be inquired about.

Some of this may sound bizarre, but that is in part because it has never been tried. By focusing intently on the idea of unlearning, we give balance to too much learning, to learning that may have occurred in the wrong way or for the wrong reasons, and to learning that should not have occurred at all. A class in unlearning would be a positive addition to every school campus; and every school campus that does not have one is depriving its students of a great educational opportunity.

DESIGNING A LEARNING CURRICULUM WHICH ADDRESSES A YOUNG PERSON'S ACTUAL LEARNING NEEDS

I believe that educators of young people must have a clear and meaningful set of teaching objectives in addition to the objective of imparting knowledge if they are going to be able to teach wisely and effectively.

One of the teaching objectives I feel all educators of young people should have is that of accommodating the need young people have to develop naturally, according to their abilities, inclinations, needs and growth patterns.

A teacher's investment of time, energy and expertise will naturally prove to be far more profitable and rewarding when the teaching tools and teaching methods employed truly harmonize with each student's development as a person, and with each student's learning interests and inclinations. As a rowboat travels easily and quickly when moving downstream, yet can have difficulty moving upstream even when manned by a competent oarsman, common sense indicates that teaching will yield the best results when the subject matter and teaching methods have been designed to harmonize with the self-development of each student, and with each student's learning interests and inclinations.

But the most important reason for teaching in harmony with each student's learning interests and inclinations is that by doing so educators are taking a strong stand in behalf of the mental and emotional well-being of their students.

All young people, be they toddlers, older teenagers, or any age in between, are engaged in a sensitive, difficult and often fragile search for themselves. Their personalities, their values, their hobbies and interests, their goals, the type of life they will live, the behavior they will manifest, the thoughts they will think, and even the feelings they will have are all in various stages of development or refinement. For this reason, the task of educating young people is an awesome and terribly important responsibility. For this reason, it is apparent to me that it is the moral responsibility of educators of young people to reinforce, support and encourage all the important and essential developmental processes occurring in their students.

Anything that is taught, and any method of teaching, which violates the various developmental processes in which all young people are engaged is unworthy of being included in the learning curriculum. Though intended to improve the minds and lives of young students, a learning curriculum cannot have redeeming value if it discourages, undermines or interferes with the natural and essential processes of self-development that are occurring in each young person.

Therefore, it is my firm belief that each learning curriculum being designed for the education of young people should be fashioned in such a way that it accommodates the essential developmental processes in which young people are engaged. To ensure that this can be accomplished in a professional and thorough manner, I suggest the introduction of a new teaching tool into the curriculum design process, for which I shall coin the term: learning profile.

An Explanation Of Learning Profiles

A learning profile is a list of a young student's learning needs, learning interests and learning inclinations, compiled so that they can be properly serviced by teachers, administrators and curriculum designers, and so that everyone connected with his education can better understand his developmental needs. A learning profile must at all times be consulted with the intent of reinforcing or strengthening a student's mental and emotional well-being. Two types of learning profiles would be helpful to have. One type would give an account of an individual student's learning needs, learning interests and learning inclinations. Another type would give an account of the learning needs, learning interests and learning inclinations of a group of students. To keep the terms simple, I shall call the first a learning profile, and the second a collective learning profile.

The value of a collective learning profile is that it can identify the particular environmental and circumstantial conditions which a group of students have in common. Students living in a farming or rural community, for example, would likely have different collective learning needs than those living in an urban setting.

By extensively researching the environmental and circumstantial conditions of a particular group of students, a detailed account of their learning needs as a group could be compiled. If a group of students were found to be severely economically disadvantaged, for example, a learning curriculum could be devised which focuses partially upon offering the students training in job skills which are immediately in demand in nearby towns. Some piecework, and work projects requiring various degrees of sophistication and expertise, could be brought in from neighboring industries to show the students the type of work that is available to them in their communities, and to develop their skills at performing it; so that they will be prepared if required to enter the work force prematurely, and so that they could begin to earn a little money on the side if they needed to. They should still be encouraged and helped to reach whatever educational goal would suit their aspirations. My suggestion simply brings a dose of realism into their immediate education.

Justification For Learning Profiles

In most human endeavors, we have a way of testing the practicality of our efforts to see if they have accomplished the intended result. Because learning has far-reaching consequences for the individual and for society, it is naturally essential that there be a way of testing the learning that students do to see if it has accomplished its intended result. The process known of as learning has a twofold intended result: that of *educating*, and that of *educating properly*. A test to see if a student has successfully memorized certain information or knowledge, which is the current method of deciding if students have accomplished one of the intended results of their studies: that of *educating*, does not determine if what has been learned has been learned in the right way, or for the right reasons; nor does it tell us if something was worthy of being learned, or if it was appropriate for a particular student to have learned it. In other words, it does not determine if a student has been *educated properly*. Thus, one of the intended results of learning has been omitted. Learning profiles, if properly compiled, will help to determine if young students are being *educated properly*.

Misuse And Origin Of Learning Profiles

If learning profiles are compiled in order to justify or reinforce existing educational practices, their reason for being

123

will have been sabotaged at the outset. There is but one purpose for the creation of learning profiles: to discover and list the actual learning needs, learning interests and learning inclinations of young students so that they can be properly serviced by teachers, administrators and curriculum designers, and so that everyone connected with their education can better understand their developmental needs.

Since learning profiles are intended to provide an accurate account of the learning needs, learning interests and learning inclinations of young students, information for the creation of learning profiles should come predominantly from students themselves. Those who design, or have input into the design, of learning curricula for young students should set aside all their preconceived notions of what young students need and want, and give them complete freedom to explain and to reveal the full extent of their learning needs and wants. Until those who design learning curricula for young students have painstakingly heard, observed and fairly analyzed the learning needs and wants of young students, they cannot know what the content of those learning needs and wants actually are; and, consequently, they cannot be adequately equipped to devise subject matter or teaching methods for properly addressing them.

Granted, educators of young students know much more than their students do about available sources and avenues which can lead a young person to become successful in life, and they can therefore be superb and effective learning resource providers. But this priceless knowledge does not make them clairvoyant. They cannot see inside the minds and hearts of their students. Because educators are no longer made of the stuff of youth, most have likely forgotten what it means to be young, and are likely out of touch with the inner concerns and needs of young people. To regain this lost knowledge so that they can effectively formulate learning curricula and teaching procedures, educators are dependent upon the input of their students regarding all aspects of their learning needs.

Prerequisites For Authoring Learning Profiles

Preparers of learning profiles must begin with a knowledge of when and how true learning occurs, and they must be clear about what should be learned.

(1) When and how does learning occur? Learning occurs the

moment a person personalizes information or knowledge. In other words, it occurs when a person adopts certain information or knowledge as his own by distilling what he wishes of it and integrating it into the way his particular mind works and into the way his particular mind is organized. To have accomplished these things, a person must have found a suitable place in his life for that information or knowledge. Learning does not occur prior to these things taking place. Simply memorizing information or knowledge, which is an incessant practice in most of today's schools, is the mere illusion of learning practiced by students to pacify teachers, parents and administrators. By itself, it accomplishes nothing. In fact, pressuring young students to memorize large amounts of information or knowledge puts a tremendous obstacle in the way of true learning. True learning requires that a sensitive, complex and personalized relationship be allowed to develop between a student and what he wishes to learn about. The most fundamental job of educators is to nurture the development of a spirited relationship between a student and an area of study or object of study which has gained his interest. The objective of this nurturing is to stimulate and encourage the impulse to learn. When a student develops a keen interest in an area of study or object of study, and becomes more and more absorbed in its many facets and possibilities, and speaks of it with great enthusiasm and deep affection, he has become imbued with the impulse to learn. No preassigned or preestablished learning curriculum can anticipate or properly address the sacred and personal nature of the impulse to learn once it has taken hold. And once the impulse to learn has become established in a student, it is important for that student to resist pressure from educators to perform learning duties or tasks which keep him from the thing or things he loves to learn about. If a young student has developed a passion for drawing, for example, educators and parents should not crowd him with history, math, English, geography and the like. Seldom is something so important to learn that it cannot wait until a student is ready to learn it. The single most important task of those who design and those who implement learning curricula for young students is to foster the impulse to learn, and then encourage it and not interfere once it has taken hold.

(2) What should be learned? Three types of things should be learned: those things which a student desires to learn; those things which are necessary for a person to learn in order to

survive in this world as an autonomous and fully functioning human; and those things which inspire us to be good and kind members of the human race. Most other things that can be learned are optional, and should not be on educators' lists of what young people should be required to learn. Teachers, administrators, parents, curriculum designers, and state and local boards of education do tremendous harm to young people by flooding their lives with things that they imagine need to be learned. Most of what teachers, educational administrators, curriculum designers, state and local boards of education and parents (when working in alliance with these authorities) think young students need to learn is unnecessary for them to learn. A history teacher thinks youngsters must learn about history; a chemistry teacher thinks youngsters should learn about chemistry; an art teacher thinks youngsters should learn such fundamentals as perspective, art history and so forth; a biology teacher thinks youngsters should learn anatomy; a teacher of literature believes youngsters should read the classics; the state and local boards of education think youngsters should be required to learn what they have devised as being "essential for all youngsters to learn;" school administrators and curriculum designers introduce yet other learning requirements – on and on it goes, to the lengths and breadths of the entire scope of knowledge; and all the frail and delicate developing youths of our land are caught up in this awful web of learning expectations and requirements, and must struggle to preserve a sense of who and what they are. If the first few frail overtures of a young student's impulse to learn arise when he is immersed in all this hubbub and pressure being imposed upon him by educators, is it surprising if they are overwhelmed and soon buried and forgotten? When are adults going to realize that with regard to the education of young people, more is not better? Just as more food is not necessarily better for the digestive system, more learning is not necessarily better for the mind and life of the young student. When it is understood by educators that, with regard to learning, more is not necessarily better, a sensible approach to formulating and designing learning curricula for young people can be possible, but not before.

Who Should Create Learning Profiles?

Learning profiles should be created by everyone concerned

with the education of young people. Learning profiles can do no harm. The more everyone knows about the learning needs, learning interests and learning inclinations of young students, the more successfully their education can be undertaken.

Each young student would benefit greatly from creating a profile of his own learning needs, learning interests and learning inclinations. It would help him to better understand his role as a student. He would also benefit from listing his positive and negative reactions to: the subject matter being offered by his teacher(s); the methods of teaching used by his teacher(s); and the educational policies of the school he attends. By comparing his assessment of his own learning needs, learning interests and learning inclinations with his positive and negative reactions to the type of education he is experiencing at the school he attends, he can see more clearly the ways in which what, and how, he is being taught at school differ from his own opinion of what his learning needs, learning interests and learning inclinations actually are. This information will be useful for him to have if he decides to request that his teacher(s), and the school he attends, be more attentive to his actual learning needs. This information can also help the student better understand his role as an active participant in the formulation and design of the type of learning he undertakes.

Curriculum designers would benefit greatly from creating individual and collective learning profiles for young students because they would then have a good way of determining the extent to which the learning curriculums they devise reflect the learning needs and aspirations of young students.

Teachers would benefit greatly from creating learning profiles for each of their students because it would enable them to understand the best ways of teaching them and improving their lives.

Parents would benefit greatly from creating learning profiles of their children's learning needs, learning interests and learning inclinations because it would help them to realize how they can be better allies of the important developmental processes in which their children are engaged. It would also enable parents to realize that educators are not necessarily the appropriate authority to consult about the proper education of their children. Parents will then begin to realize that it is often their children who know the best courses of action to take in pursuit of their own learning, in spite of the likelihood that they may have inadequate abilities of articulating them.

127

Learning Profiles Must Be Validated By Students

To be legitimate and accurate, a profile of a young student's learning needs, learning interests and learning inclinations that has been created by someone other than the student must be validated by the student. The student must examine it carefully, perhaps discuss it with his teacher(s), parents and peers, make needed changes to it, and finally agree that its contents accurately describes his learning needs, learning interests and learning inclinations. As time passes, he may wish to revise it.

A teacher who has created a profile of a particular student's learning needs, learning interests and learning inclinations must obtain the student's feedback about it before she can be guided by it in her teaching efforts. Once a teacher has been assured that her assessment of the learning needs, learning interests and learning inclinations of a particular student appears to be accurate because it has been validated by the student, she can proceed in instructing with a good deal of confidence. She should then be able to clearly perceive one or more avenues or approaches for helping the student learn those things which will genuinely benefit and help him or her.

Learning Profiles For An Entire Classroom

Any teacher who likes the idea of creating profiles of the learning needs, learning interests and learning inclinations of her students can begin to do so in the following manner which has occurred to me, but which I'm sure is but one of many good ways that could be devised to do so.

At the beginning of the school semester, the teacher would ask all her students (or all her students in a single class) to help her better understand their learning needs, learning interests and learning inclinations so that she can teach more appealing subjects and so that she can teach in a manner that harmonizes with their own idea of how they would like to participate in the learning process. The teacher would ask her students to write down, as honestly and completely as possible, the things each of them would like to learn, and the manner in which they would feel most comfortable participating in the learning process. The students should be asked if they would be interested in experimenting with different methods of learning, and if they would be interested in being exposed to subjects different from what they are currently studying, and if they feel the time spent in any aspect of the learning they have been doing is excessive or unnecessary; and they should be asked to explain their answers in as much detail as possible. They should be asked to list their learning goals for themselves, and any special problems they have in reaching them. Allowing time for reflection, the process may take a few days. The students should be told that this information would be kept confidential; and only the teacher would have it, unless the students choose to reveal it to others. The students should be told that statements they make in this exercise would not be used against them, and would not affect their grades. The information gathered from this effort would generate other questions, which the teacher could ask her students at another time.

Students Should Critique Teachers And Schools

Since the learning needs, learning interests and learning inclinations of young students can be stimulated, aided and encouraged, or frustrated and undermined, by their teachers and by the policies of the schools they attend, it is important that all young students be provided an opportunity to periodically critique their teachers and the policies of the schools they attend. And since a student's involvement in the learning he or she undertakes can be more clearly understood in connection with these critiques, student critiques of their teachers and schools should be near at hand when examining the learning profiles of the students so that both can be studied simultaneously. Student critiques of their teachers and schools should not affect their grades, nor the way they are treated by their teachers or school administrators.

Many approaches could be devised for obtaining student critiques of their teachers and schools. The content of those critiques will be determined in large part by the degree of freedom given the students in this effort and by the selection of questions posed to the students. To encourage a complete and unfettered account of their feelings about the quality of their teachers and schools, I would ask students to answer the following list of questions, which could be amended as needed.

(1) Do you feel the education you have received at this school until now has been the best that it could be? If not the best, how could it be improved?

(2) Do you feel the education you have received at this school until now has helped you or hurt you, or have you been

helped by it in some ways and hurt by it in others? Please explain your answer.

(3) Do you feel the teaching methods used by your teachers, and the policies of this school, bring out your best learning efforts or frustrate them? Please explain your answer.

(4) Are you expected or required to learn things at this school that you feel do not benefit you or are a nuisance, and do you feel you could be learning other things instead which could be of greater value to you or of greater interest to you? Please explain your comments.

(5) Do you feel the teachers in this school understand what people of your age need and want from their teachers? Which teachers are supportive of your educational aims and interests, and which ones undermine them or interfere with your pursuit of them?

(6) Do you feel your teachers and school administrators should try to better understand your needs and wants so that your school will be a happier, healthier and more useful place in which to spend your time?

(7) What subjects and methods of teaching do you feel would suit you better than the ones now in vogue at your school?

(8) How can the learning environment at your school be improved to enable you to become a more dedicated and skilled learner?

(9) Do you sometimes feel that too much emphasis is placed on learning, and that more time and effort should be spent on just living your life instead?

(10) If you owned the school you attend, or were its principal, how would you run it differently so that the students at the school could receive a good education and a happy one?

What Would Learning Profiles Accomplish?

If profiles of young students' learning needs, learning interests and learning inclinations were obtained, and were then seriously evaluated by teachers and administrators; and if teachers and administrators then heeded and abided by the many insights and evaluations they garnered from doing so, it would lead to the following consequences.

(1) Teachers and administrators could be held more accountable for the psychological and emotional well-being of their students, which would make them become better

educators.

(2) There would be a means of determining when the learning activities of young students violate the important and essential processes of self-development in which they are engaged.

(3) There would be a means of separating the learning activities which are useful and pleasing to each young student from those which are not; and of spotting the general aspects of the educational process which are irrelevant or inimical to the needs of young students.

(4) There would be a means of personalizing the educational process and of tailoring it to better suit the needs of each student.

(5) It would allow students to have much more say about the kind of education they receive.

(6) It would allow a natural and reinforcing educational methodology to evolve.

(7) It would infuse into the educational process a spirit of experimentation for the purpose of enriching the learning, teaching and administrative experiences of those who are most intimately involved in the education of young students.

Conclusion

The primary purpose of this paper has been to make a case for greater student participation in the learning process. I believe that no limits should be placed upon the degree to which young students are allowed to regain control of the choices connected with what they are to learn and how they are to learn. Young people should be given every opportunity to prove that they can learn without being compelled or pressured to do so. Educators and parents must learn to have faith in what young people are all about. They must learn to give young students credit for having fine sensibilities. They must believe that young students want to prepare themselves to become competent and capable individuals, and that they will make a great effort to do so if provided with good learning opportunities and good learning resources. They must believe that young students, themselves, and not teachers, administrators or curriculum designers, are the ones who are best able to discover what they need to learn and when they need to learn it.

THE INDEPENDENT TEACHER

In order to be paid a salary, the teachers of our youngsters conform. They conform when they attend a college or university to get their teaching credential. And they conform when they teach within guidelines set by their state and local school boards and by the school in which they teach.

Conforming is not always bad. We conform to laws which protect our civil rights, for example, and that is good. But when large numbers of qualified and certified teachers have to conform to educational policies and practices which stifle their teaching creativity, or undermine their teaching autonomy, the entire system for educating young people in this country is suspect, and should be thoroughly investigated for incompetence and evil doings.

There is no merit in certifying teachers if that certification does not entitle them to teach in the ways they deem appropriate to the needs of their students. If it is thought that not all certified teachers are equally mature or equally able to perform their professional duties, various levels or degrees of certification should be established which permit increased teaching autonomy as it becomes warranted. But there must be some level of certification which entitles teachers to virtually complete autonomy in what they teach their students and how they teach them.

What incentive can there be for a teacher who tries to find out how best to educate her students; and, upon coming to some conclusions on the matter and enacting them, discovers that her choice of subject matter or teaching methods are not permitted according to state, local or institutional guidelines, or must be significantly diluted or modified because of them? The answer is simple. There is no incentive to teach if a teacher's best professional judgment about what to teach and how to teach cannot be employed.

A teacher must put forth her best teaching effort according to the principles and procedures she feels are correct if: she is going to feel good about her job; her students are going to view her as having genuineness and integrity; she is going to be able to generate proper feedback from her students regarding her success in teaching them. If the subject matter and teaching methods a teacher employs do not come from her mind and heart, she cannot be personally involved in the success or failure of her students. If the subject matter and teaching methods she employs were not fully endorsed by her, she will not regard herself as responsible for the learning efforts of her students or for the outcome of those efforts.

In my opinion, a good teacher is one who has a deep sense of what she wants to teach, how she wants to teach and why she wants to teach; and will not permit her teaching talents to be diluted, her teaching goals to be undermined or her teaching methods to be modified by state or local educational authorities, or by administrators of the school in which she teaches. It is only insights into the learning needs and living circumstances of her students that will guide and instruct her as a teacher. A teacher cannot serve two different masters at the same time. She cannot service the needs of her students and the needs of her employer (the school) simultaneously unless they are synonymous or closely aligned; but they often are not. Every teacher must decide to teach in the best interests of her students, according to her best professional understanding of what should be taught them, and how they should be taught. This is a teacher's greatest burden and most noble calling. If she can succeed at adhering to it, she has a good chance of fulfilling her mission of becoming a successful educator. Otherwise, she will fall far short of that objective, and may very likely acquire increasing amounts of regret as she continues to teach.

It is a teacher's moral and professional obligation to teach in the manner he or she feels is best for each student, and to teach those things each student is interested in learning; even if it means defying the learning requirements mandated by state and local school boards, the local school district authorities, and the administrators of the school in which she teaches. I realize that it is terrible to have to jeopardize one's job in order to teach as one's conscience dictates, and that putting one's job on the line for the sake of one's students would require great courage; but if more teachers were willing to do it, perhaps the higher authorities responsible for educational procedures and policies would eventually fall into line, and begin themselves to work in the best interests of the students.

In a compulsory system of education, in which students must perform in ways that are required of them, teachers become enforcers. They are hired to ensure that education occurs in the forms that are acceptable to those who pay their salaries. They are required to measure a student's progress according to standards of performance provided to them by their employer. When a teacher accepts a salary, she usually, at least partially, mortgages her integrity of purpose to her employer, who describes to her many aspects of the form in which her teaching must manifest itself. It is understood by everyone in the working world that an employee must conform to the expectations and requirements of his employer while on the job; but there are certain professions in which complete autonomy and complete genuineness are essential in order to perform the duties inherent in the job. Teaching is one of those professions. There are certain professions in which the quality of the service rendered or the quality of the work performed can be severely undermined or corrupted by employer guidelines or restraints. Teaching is such a profession.

Teaching requires great flexibility to the changing needs of the student, and spontaneous decision making on a daily basis, if it is to be effective. Virtually any model or structure which a teacher is required to follow concerning the subject matter offered to students, or methods of teaching them, will prove to be a source of interference.

As long as teachers are forced to obey teaching guidelines and restraints given them by their employer (the school), or given them indirectly by some educational agency such as a state or local school board, teaching can never be a wholly honorable profession. When a teacher's employer (the school) insists that she teach within prescribed guidelines or according to certain learning prerequisites, which have been fashioned or condoned by state and local educational authorities, and the teacher complies in order to pacify her employer and retain her job, the teacher has become a tool society uses to impose its will upon youngsters. In this context, when parents entrust their children to a school, they are in effect entrusting them to the wishes of the state, and the teacher is an agent of the state which enacts its will upon the child. Thus, children are being molded in the image of the state by paid agents called teachers. The parent then is the accomplice of the state. Teachers working in such an environment, who wish still to be sincere and dedicated teachers, must attempt to do so within the time and space not used by what the school, the school boards, and the local school authorities require of them. This is not fair to the teachers, nor to their students; and can be superfluous if what is required of teachers by their superiors contradicts their (the teachers') sense of what is best for their students.

It is interesting that there are often teacher strikes for higher salaries, but rarely for greater teaching autonomy. It would be far nobler for teachers to go on strike for total autonomy in their teaching than for an increase in pay, and it would be of far greater benefit to the students they instruct.

I feel it is incumbent upon the teaching profession to dissolve the authority of the state and local school boards, and the authority of school districts and of the schools themselves, to dictate teaching procedures, or to decide what subject matter must be taught. A teacher who has been fully certified should be able to teach what she wants, as she wants and when she wants, so long as she can *prove, or provide convincing evidence*, that she is fulfilling the learning needs of the students she is assigned to teach.

And how can we decide if a teacher is fulfilling the learning needs of the students he or she is assigned to teach? I can think of only one way: by asking the students, and by observing how they are progressing with their lives. If a teacher's students are happy in school and flourishing; if they are expanding their awareness and understanding; if the character traits they demonstrate are praiseworthy; and if they are continuously learning; then the teacher is doing a beautiful job and a good one. It is the state and local school boards, the local school district authorities and the policies of schools themselves that are intervening and interfering in what the teacher is able to do for the student; thereby disabling the teaching process and draining it of its genuineness. I'm for giving the job of teaching back to the teachers, where it belongs and has always belonged.

In saying all that I have said, I do not wish to exclude educational administrators from the educational process. I feel there is a place in the education of youngsters for everyone who truly cares about their well-being and development. I guess I am advocating a change of roles for educational administrators. I would prefer to see their roles as being supportive of the needs of teachers and students, instead of being authoritative and controlling in nature, as they currently are.

WHAT SHOULD BE THE ROLE OF THE TEACHER OF CHILDREN?

While adults have specific reasons for attending school, and do so voluntarily; children attend school at the request of their elders, and often under pressure to do so. While adults may at any time quit a school, or a particular class or learning program within a school they attend, children usually may not. Clearly, children are placed in a school, and expected to participate in the programs of a school, without their consent. Their wishes are not consulted, nor is a proper investigation made of their learning or developmental needs, before beginning to teach them. They are herded through programs at the behest of educators, and at the convenience of educators. Little, if any, attempt is made to determine the effects of this blatant manipulation.

Adults have long assumed it is their moral duty to manipulate and mold children insofar as their education is concerned because they worry that if they do not establish a direction for children by steering them and nudging them, cajoling them and pressuring them – thus controlling their lives as students, children will not develop properly. Adults, on the whole, have transferred responsibility for this objective onto professional educators, who oversee their children's education in the aforesaid authoritarian manner.

The fact that children are vulnerable, pliable and usually unquestioning of the authority of their elders does not entitle professional educators to impose learning upon them. Professional educators may assume they have the right to impose learning upon children to ensure that they become properly educated, and parents may believe educators should have this right; but, in reality, no one has the right to demand learning of children. It is a gross violation of their civil rights.

Making children learn is as inappropriate as making your friend go for a walk, or making your friend climb a tree, or making your friend cut your front lawn. All people, of all ages, respond extremely poorly to being forced to do things. It is not in human nature to be forced, manipulated or controlled. It is contrary to every decent concept of democracy and of freedom. The moment you force someone to do something, you assume the role of dictator. The role of dictator may be required in emergencies and to ensure children's safety, but it should not be used as a method of teaching children.

Since most children are not asking for formal education, but are simply obliging their elders by going to school, it is extremely important for parents to make sure educators are not imposing or dictatorial hosts while their children are in their care. If educators impose upon children in unfair ways, thereby generating hostility and resentment in children, it would not be surprising if children held their parents to be partly responsible because they are attending school to please them. This hostility and resentment toward their parents may be of an unconscious variety, but real nonetheless.

The most important idea to keep in mind when educating children is the fact that *all children are immersed in sensitive, complex and critical patterns of self-development.* Their formal education cannot occur properly if it is inharmonious with their various patterns of self-development. Consequently, the primary role of the teacher of children must be that of fitting what he or she has to offer into the self-development of children. The only way this can be accomplished is for the education of children to cease being an educator-centered process, and to begin being a student-centered process.

But today, most public and private schools for the education of children are educator-centered. The programs, devices, concoctions, and whims of educators are central and all-important. Little effort is made to determine the degree to which children need, want or can properly participate in what educators force upon them. In today's scheme of educating children, the educator is a dictator and children are his or her pawns. Gains that are made in acquiring information under this scheme are often losses with respect to the personal identity and overall development of the individual student.

To reverse this process, and begin to establish a solid foundation for the education of children, reasonable minds must prevail. The old ways of doing things must be discarded. Only those who have the courage to begin anew, with new concepts and new methods should step forward to reform and rebuild our institutions for educating our children.

I believe the new instructor of children must first determine if the students in her charge require, or can use, her services. Secondly, the instructor must nurture in the students a willingness or desire to be taught by her. In other words, the new teacher of children must first justify her teaching. And that is because her students likely have not elected to learn from her. They are simply obliging their parents by being in school.

A period of initial adjustment to this unnatural situation must precede the instruction of children. This period of initial adjustment will address the civil rights of the students, and the professional rights of the teacher.

The civil rights of children are centered in their right to refuse being manipulated, even for so noble a purpose as education. We all know that an employer has a right to manipulate his employees within certain parameters in order to get the job done that he is paying them to do. But our society has erred in assuming that educators have a mandate, or a right, to demand learning of children in their charge.

A thoughtful analysis of this issue will reveal that demanding learning of children is inappropriate in a majority of cases. It humiliates children, frightens them, intimidates them, disorients them, and often establishes in them resentment and hostility toward learning.

Demanding learning of children is also an unfair assignment for teachers. Teachers placed in the position of having to demand learning from children are themselves given an ignoble task. It can be humiliating, unrewarding and demoralizing.

In conclusion, the entire foundational theory upon which the teaching of children has been established must be thoroughly reexamined. Much of it is destructive of the aims of a free and healthy society. Much of it is clearly undemocratic.

If demanding learning of children violates their civil rights and is unfair to teachers, what should be the precise role of the teacher of children?

I suggest that the role of the teacher of children should be limited to that of a facilitator who is not permitted to demand learning of her students. She can suggest learning, encourage learning, and make it possible for learning to occur. She is then a gatherer of educational resources and materials, a provider of an educational environment, and a personal source of inspiration, support and encouragement for her students.

If a teacher of children is not permitted to demand learning of her students, her students need not participate in her programs, offerings or suggestions. This sends an important signal to the teacher. It tells the teacher that she must win her students over by genuine teaching skills, and by genuine human qualities. If she is to develop a proper teacher-student relationship, she must learn how to properly address the learning and developmental needs of her students, and she must have personal qualities which her students find appealing. The students themselves will determine if she is a successful instructor by their voluntary responses to her, and to her teaching efforts.

A school which wholeheartedly advocates, and practices, voluntary learning for children in all instances, and at all times, sends an important signal to those who design and mandate learning curricula. It would appear at the outset that their specialized services are not needed. But perhaps this is not entirely the case. Certainly, if all schools for children were places of voluntary learning, there would no longer be any mandated learning curricula; but perhaps there could still exist specialists who design learning curricula. Their work as curriculum designers would then require different research than is commonly used for such a purpose, and much more personal involvement with the lives and needs of children. The new brand of curriculum designers would likely have to do a good deal of on-site field work to see how well their *suggested* curricula is being used, and to see if it is being used at all. Their success as curriculum designers would be predicated upon the frequency with which their *suggested* programs, projects and materials are voluntarily accessed, and upon their appeal to students.

Schools, teachers, curriculum designers and educational administrators may wish to straddle the fence *between* methods of instruction which favor mandatory learning for children and those which favor voluntary learning for children. In other words, they may advocate and practice a mixture of the two educational methods simultaneously. With regards to instructing children, I suggest that this is like trying to mix oil with water.

Children need and deserve a learning atmosphere, or environment, devoid of the tyranny of curriculum enforcement. Educators need to show children what they know to be true: that something as invigorating, inspiring and useful as learning need not be required or enforced. By teaching children a love of learning using genuine teaching skills and genuine human qualities, and by gently fostering – within a resource-rich educational environment – the dynamic impulse to learn which resides in embryonic form in every child, children can be stimulated and encouraged to attempt voluntary learning of all types and varieties. They will then automatically regard

139

learning as their lifelong helpmate and benefactor, and willingly immerse themselves in it.

When educators teach children that the love of learning is an insufficient motivation for learning by pressuring them and cajoling them to learn what they (the educators) have predetermined is best for them to learn, educators destroy in children the inclination to develop both a love of learning and a love of knowledge at the very beginning of their lives, which is when they most need to acquire them. On the other hand, if the concept of voluntary learning for children is properly researched and implemented, it will restore a love of learning and a love of knowledge to the lives of all children, and stimulate and invigorate the learning process in unforeseen and glorious ways.

Compulsory education for children has been tried for such a long time, and has so often failed the teachers and the children, or produced mixed or uncertain results, that it is now time to try voluntary learning for children in its most undiluted form. Although the idea of voluntary learning for children in a completely undiluted form might seem extreme, it is actually a very basic and logical approach to educating children. In the beginning, *pilot programs* should be tried, but only in an undiluted form. No admixture of compulsory, required or mandated exercises or programs should accompany them, infiltrate them or be interwoven into them. This is the only way in which this method of teaching children can be properly instituted, and properly evaluated by teachers, students, curriculum designers and educational administrators.

AN IMPARTER OF KNOWLEDGE

Besides having a large quantity of knowledge in their areas of expertise, usually far more than their students have, teachers also know such things as how to effectively organize the subject matter they instruct; what the preferred learning tools and resources are in their areas of expertise, and how best to access them; and can likely suggest some effective learning procedures within their areas of expertise. A teacher who has all these skills would certainly seem qualified to impart knowledge to students, which is the primary function of teachers in today's schools.

In today's schools, a good teacher is regarded as a trusted and infallible guide capable of leading his or her students along a treacherous mountain trail that leads to knowledge, or safely through an unmarked wilderness of confusing concepts and unrelated data. This view of the teacher's role establishes the teacher as one who is all-seeing and all-knowing; and the final authority on the content of what is to be learned, as well as the procedures for learning it. What, if anything, is wrong with this concept of teaching?

I believe the problem with this concept of teaching is that the mental make-up and natural response patterns of the learner are not being taken into account; or, if acknowledged, are not being taken seriously enough. Unless the learner is feigning attention or participation, teaching is always an intrusion (either welcomed or unwelcomed by the learner) upon the order and content of the mind of the learner. I believe that one of the primary responsibilities of the teacher is to respect, and cater to, the mental make-up and natural response patterns of the learner. What is being taught, and how it is being taught, is not as important as how the learner is responding to it.

There can be nothing more personal in a person's life than the contents of his or her mind. I believe that no one has the right to intrude upon the order or content of a person's mind without being given at least tacit permission each step of the way. I believe that the points at which the learner's interest in what the teacher is offering wanes, or ceases altogether, the teacher should grant the learner immunity from instruction. To be effective, teaching must be a collaborative effort between the teacher and learner; and when the learner ceases to be a willing partner in that collaboration, further instruction can only breed resentment in the learner. In other words, teaching should be done by invitation only. As the prominent American educator, John Holt, has said, "Uninvited teaching does not make learning. For the most part, such teaching prevents learning."[1]

This truth is best seen in the conversation patterns between people. When two people are talking to one another, each is temporarily extending a welcoming ear to the other. However, this can change quickly. One moment we are pleased or satisfied with an ongoing conversation in which we are a participant, and the next minute we are bored with it or simply have had enough of it. We then disengage our self, or pretend a lingering interest out of courtesy for as short a time as we can manage. But we always know the precise points at which it is no longer comfortable or appropriate for us to remain engaged in the conversation; and if we were compelled to continue in the conversation beyond the point of our choosing to, we would resent it greatly.

I believe that the natural response patterns of people are the key to establishing sound teaching and learning practices. To be happy and productive learners, students require flexibility to shift the focus of their attention at will, and to change their degree and manner of involvement at will, in their learning activities. When permitted this degree of learning flexibility, students may challenge a teacher's reasoning, or express disappointment or disinterest in a teacher's lectures or offerings. In the process of doing so, they may be sparked in a different learning direction equally as valuable as the one suggested by the teacher, but of greater personal significance. Let me give an example.

While attending college, I recall times when I was in disagreement with my teacher's ideas, or radically branched off from them in my thinking. Often I was unable, or unwilling, to stay focused on the professor's subject or line of reasoning; but it sometimes aroused in me interest in another direction. Once that interest was aroused, I felt an obligation to respond to it, and resented it when class demands upon my time prevented me from doing so. In a class I was taking in behavioral psychology, I found the impersonal approach to the human repugnant; but in opposing it, I stumbled upon the works of Abraham Maslow in the college library. I wanted time to pursue reading and research related to his work, and I wanted to discuss his ideas in class. However, since that wasn't permitted, and since I had similar problems in other classes, I stopped attending the college. I'm sure many learning careers were cut short for similar or comparable reasons, simply because the natural response patterns of the learner were not encouraged in the classes.

A couple of years ago, I attended a large beginning computer class. It was a twenty week, Saturday course, with optional 4 or 8 hours attendance. Everyone worked from the same step by step self-study book, which was the basis of the course. The age range of the class was from high school to senior citizens. The teacher was concerned that the younger students make something of themselves, and occasionally gave the whole class a pep talk about not wasting time in class. The teacher's role was as a problem solver when students ran into difficulties understanding the book, or their computer. It appeared that every student was a willing participant who wanted to become knowledgeable in the usage of the computer; but the students were not willing and eager participants at every moment, or to the same degree, or with regards to the same aspects of what they were learning. Their interest increased or waned as their reactions dictated. At the points at which their interest waned, their participation lessened or stopped altogether. When their interest picked up, their participation increased. This is as it should be. When their interest waned, some of the students resorted to playing Solitaire on their computers, or doing other non-class-related activities on their computers. Were they wasting time, or just attending to their personal needs? I believe they were attending to their personal needs; and that, luckily for them, the teacher for the most part turned a blind eye to these activities because he realized, perhaps instinctively, that uninvited teaching does not make learning.

Recently I attended a one-session class in critical thinking in which the teacher, Kathy Brown, was a moderator learning along with her students. The students were given the opportunity to be coequal with the teacher in guiding the direction of the class, and eagerly seized that opportunity. Even though the teacher was more informed on the subject than the students, the input of all the participants created the structure of the class and guided its direction. Certain leaders emerged from the class because they held the strongest opinions on the subject. The best ideas dominated the session. No one knew the direction the class would ultimately go in, including the teacher.

Besides participating as a coequal learner, the teacher sometimes offered ideas or questions to keep the discussion moving; but it was only when the participation of the students died down, and seemed in danger of coming to a halt, that she felt obligated to lead.

Kathy's role as teacher in the class on critical thinking was non-authoritarian and non-intrusive. I believe that whole subject areas could be addressed in the same way, at all grade levels; and that, if properly planned and executed, students could move along in their learning quite effectively without the pressure of grades, monitoring or assignments to interfere with their natural learning inclinations and natural response patterns. In this scenario, the teacher would cease being an imparter of knowledge, and would become a sharer of knowledge. The students would be free to tap into the teacher's knowledge for their own purposes; and would be encouraged to determine the direction of their studies as well as the style of their participation in class. The teacher would be flexible to the students' changing needs, and would make sure the class is a haven for diverse learning interests and approaches. Can such a learning and teaching model be as effective as, or more effective than, traditional methods of schooling? There's only one way to find out: try it!

[1] Learning All the Time by John Holt

THREE KINDS OF LEARNING

There are three different kinds of learning that commonly occur. One kind is the learning that occurs for personal gratification or personal fulfillment. It includes learning which aids one's self-development, learning voluntarily undertaken to improve one's understanding, and learning for the love of knowledge. A second kind of learning consists of mastering a specific body of knowledge or acquiring specific skills, under pressure and in an allotted period of time, for financial or commercial objectives. A third kind of learning is for the sole purpose of satisfying the expectations of educators.

As adults in a modern society, we are all aware that the job market is fiercely competitive; and that to earn a good living, we must master a trade or skill, or become expert in a body of knowledge. To accomplish this second kind of learning, we know we must subject ourselves to hard work and discipline over a sustained period of time. We know we will be required to be practical, efficient, matter-of-fact and responsible. Often there will not be much time to reflect upon, to negotiate, or to be choosy about the learning process itself, or its personal effects upon us. We will be called upon to meet this deadline or that schedule, to undertake this assignment or that project. These things are all part of the instructor's or school's guarantee to make us proficient in the skills or body of knowledge we have signed up for in a specified period of time.

Confusing the three kinds of learning contaminates the educational process, and makes it unwholesome and ineffective. I believe most educators and schools approach the educational process in a lopsided manner because they conceive of it as being one-dimensional. They see clearly the second kind of learning: learning to master a body of knowledge or specific skills for financial or commercial objectives in an allotted period of time; but they do not fully understand the significance of learning for self-development, understanding, or for the love of knowledge.

The great error educators and schools make is in assuming that learning for personal gratification or personal fulfillment (including learning for self-development, understanding, and for the love of knowledge) is an inferior type of learning that should be thought of as a hobby, or spare time pursuit. The opposite is true. Learning undertaken to acquire skills or a body of knowledge, under pressure and in an allotted period of time, for financial or commercial objectives, is the kind of learning that is of secondary value. The third kind of learning, learning simply to satisfy the expectations of educators, has no redeeming value.

It is time for everyone in the profession of educating others to concede that most learning that occurs under pressure, in order to meet deadlines or fulfill the requirements of a course of study, is a form of harassment. Sometimes the harassment is mild, but more likely it is substantial or severe. If an adult is willing to put himself at the mercy of that type of learning for a limited period of time to gain proficiency at certain skills, or to acquire a specified body of knowledge, the adult is surely entitled to do so. And no one can question the fact that a practical purpose has been served when the goal is achieved. But the process by which the adult acquired the skills or body of knowledge is antithetical to good learning habits because it is impersonal and offensive to the developmental process.

Ideally, the human mind should never be placed on an assembly line, where it can be modified or improved upon at will by teachers, or by others acting in the capacity of educator. True learning is a growing process, subject to all the principles of growth and development. True learning is a reaching out and connecting. It is the slow process of selecting, absorbing and understanding. It cannot be rushed or forced. Education that is worth the name must cater to the human mind: to its needs and wants, its intricacies, its inclinations and foibles.

When learning bypasses our curiosity, our enthusiasm and our sympathies, or gives only feeble or half-hearted attention to them; when the subject matter and not the degree and manner of our personal involvement is what is important; it is obvious that our self-unfoldment and personal enrichment are not the focus. And it is obvious that learning for the sake of the complete man (or woman), and for the sake of the good society, is being compromised or ignored altogether.

It is wrong to compare the businesslike pursuit of learning with learning which caters to the personal needs of the individual. One summons forth the talents, abilities, idiosyncrasies and uniqueness of the individual; and in the end produces a great society. The other buries the individual in a flurry of efforts to satisfy an expected result. The one nurtures the mind's unfoldment, while the other seeks only to attach to the mind a trade or skill or body of knowledge.

146

PROFESSIONAL EDUCATORS HAVE FAILED OUR CHILDREN

Compulsory education for children is a worldwide phenomenon. Sometimes it is politically motivated, in order to produce a certain kind of citizen. Sometimes it is religiously motivated, in order to indoctrinate young minds in the teachings and beliefs of a particular faith. Sometimes it is financed directly or indirectly by business and industry to ensure that there will be future generations of willing workers and trained manpower. Sometimes it functions as a babysitting service for working parents. It can exist to perpetuate the monetary gain of educators, educational administrators and publishers of learning materials. It can exist to satisfy the well-meaning expectations of adults, regardless of how far-fetched and arbitrary those expectations might be. Lastly, it can exist solely for the benefit of children. Even when compulsory education benefits children overall, and I believe those instances are the exception rather than the rule, its benefits may be short-lived, and may fall short of what is best for children. In fact, all the uses of compulsory education for children are suspect, and most endanger the well being and development of children in many important ways.

It's easy to understand how the theory of compulsory education, even in its most altruistic form, was conceived, and why its originators misconstrued its essence. Adults, on the whole, want the best for their children and for all children. They know from experience that life is difficult, and that young people had best be prepared insofar as possible for the problems that lie ahead. And they are concerned that children be given proper guidance and proper training to succeed in life. And so, somewhere along the road of human history, adults came up with the idea of interceding in the development of children because they thought that with all of their adult wisdom, experience and skills, surely they could do a better job preparing children for their future lives than Mother Nature, when left to her own devices. And, with these ideas in mind, adults invented the school. And then they devised teacher-training institutes to prepare teachers to teach in schools. Of course, a school for teachers must provide methods of instruction, and so theories of education were born. Since subject matter would be needed in schools, the idea of curriculum was born, and with that curriculum designers came into being. And Boards of Education were devised to oversee the whole process, which by that time had gotten to be complex and unwieldy.

At first it seemed like a great cause. Important people worked hard for it, lobbied for it, and even donated their own money to the great cause of Formal Education. Then Government got involved in a big way, and helped create innumerable schools and innumerable teacher-training institutes. Many adults were naturally hopeful that the great experiment of compulsory instruction for children would turn out to be a great boon to the children as well as to society.

But instead of aiding the development of children, the great cause of formal, compulsory instruction has meddled in unfortunate and innumerable ways. It has woefully and wrongly tampered with children's lives. Countless children have been thrown off the train tracks which nature provided, and which would have led them to happiness and success in life, and professional educators don't know how to put children back on the tracks which nature provided. Rather than admit the error of their ways, professional educators have turned to drugging children in large numbers to keep them compliant. Plainly and simply, professional educators of children have misconstrued the essence and nature of their job. Their arrogance, which is revealed *in granting themselves authority to determine the learning needs and wants of youngsters, and in manipulating their learning,* has gotten the world's children into a lot of trouble. Professional educators have toyed with Mother Nature, and have failed terribly because their original assumptions of how best to educate children were wrong, very wrong. Instilled in them were the seeds of devastating failure, which were destined to sprout once planted.

To show how professional educators of children have gone wrong, let us first look at the mind of the child. It is fragile, susceptible, impressionable and vulnerable. It requires proper conditions and beneficial influences to develop properly. Just as all species nurture and protect their young during their time of vulnerability and susceptibility, one of our foremost responsibilities as humans is to nurture and protect children during their formative years. How educators interpret that responsibility will determine if they are friends of the children they teach or hostile intruders into their lives.

Every educator of children should be asked to answer the

following question before receiving a credential to teach them: "How can an educator nurture and protect the mind of the child?" Failure to provide an appropriate answer should disallow their credential or revoke it. I believe most educators of children have not thought through the question; or if they have thought about it, they have not come up with conclusions which are either valid or sensible. The methods of instructing children used in schools indicate that most educators of children would fail the question.

To come up with appropriate answers to the question of how best to nurture and protect the mind of the child, the following question must be considered: "Should the mind of a child be formed by others, or should it be given the proper environment in which to become formed in its own way, perhaps even to form itself?" It is the failure of educators to consider the full breadth and depth of that question which has caused them to become hostile intruders into the lives of the children they educate. Where educators of children have gone wrong is in adopting the simplistic and error-laden idea that it is the responsibility of educators to form the mind of the child, instead of providing an appropriate learning environment in which the mind of the child could become formed in its own way.

What the educators of children have failed to take into account are the developmental needs of children. They have attempted to educate children in the same way they educate adults: *by prescribing subject matter for them, requiring them to learn it, and regulating many of the terms and conditions of the learning process.* Since the minds of children are fragile, impressionable, vulnerable and susceptible, they can be over-powered, intimidated and controlled by this method of teaching, which is why it is dangerous, unhealthy and unethical. When applied to the education of children, this method of teaching is also undemocratic, and a form of brainwashing and indoctrination. It is important to note that there is little difference in method in teaching Chinese children Maoist doctrines or American children American History if enforcement and intimidation accompany the teaching of them.

Sound ideas of child psychology must be at the foundation of any sensible attempt to educate children. Within every child are the seeds of certain personality characteristics, talents, abilities, idiosyncrasies and so forth. Every child inherits different living circumstances. Educators need to be taught that

149

their foremost responsibility is to work with the uniqueness of each child, and with each child's unique circumstances, so that the child might develop in the way nature intended. Bypassing the uniqueness of each child, or pretending it is unimportant, or thinking that it will have the strength to continue developing normally within predesigned programs of mass instruction is foolhardy. The moment professional educators impose a set of learning conditions on children, either by enforcement or intensive persuasion, they endanger the sensitive developmental processes which are ongoing in the mind of every child. Educators must protect the mind of the child from being brainwashed, indoctrinated or manipulated so that it can find a path of self-development which is suitable to it and agreeable. To accomplish this, the learning that children do must become optional and voluntary instead of compulsory or required.

Compulsory education accomplishes the opposite of what it intends. Instead of guaranteeing children will learn, it guarantees they will resent learning and rebel. Perhaps the most fundamental part of being human is the urge to rebel when told what to do. Rebelling against being told what to do is at the heart of every legitimate concept of liberty and democracy. To train children that the way to learn is through submission and obedience is to train them for slavery, not freedom. It contradicts not only sound principles of child development, of individuality, but also of democracy and freedom.

The practice of demanding learning from children, of forcing education upon them, is itself an admission of the failure to educate. People who are desperate to gain the results they want, and who are unskilled in obtaining them, resort to enforcement. Compulsory education for children is clearly undemocratic. It uses the tools of the dictator: intimidation, punishment, reprimand, subordination to authority, rules of compliance. These are awful tools and should be used upon criminals and tyrants, not upon the fragile and vulnerable minds of our children!

If educators of children have courage and wisdom, and are able to admit to making mistakes, they would be willing to attempt educating children without the use of any mandated or required curricula, and without any mandated or required programs, tests or assignments. There are long-existing, and very successful models of this educational method. Three such examples are: Sudbury Valley School, Framingham, MA; Summerhill School, Suffolk, England; Windsor House Public

School, Vancouver, British Columbia, Canada. These schools are remarkable examples of how best to educate children. They are noble efforts, achieved by means of the great sacrifice, endurance and vision of their founders. I believe that educators who neglect to thoroughly investigate the methods of these schools cannot know what is best for children. Perhaps the single most important lesson these schools have for educators is the example they demonstrate daily that as all mandatory curricula and all required learning are eliminated from the instruction of children (provided the proper educational environment, learning resources and learning opportunities are offered to them), their learning becomes vigorous and genuine, and begins to blossom in unforeseen and glorious ways, a pleasure for all to behold and to accommodate.

Voluntary learning for children does not mean depriving the child of learning opportunities or of an educational environment rich in educational resources; nor does it mean depriving the child of the assistance of willing and capable mentors and instructors. Voluntary learning for children does not mean inviting chaos or anarchy into the school. If properly understood and properly instituted, voluntary learning for children is viable and practical, and it is the correct way to educate children.

In fairness to educators of children, one can conclude they have simply overlooked certain important issues relevant to educating children, and have allowed themselves to be swept downstream by current educational fads, procedures and methods. That fact does not disallow the seriousness of their errors, nor does it hold them less accountable for them, but it does make them understandable. We can all make mistakes, and if the educators of children would only be willing to look at the critical mistakes they are making, it is not too late to correct them.

UNSCHOOLING

In addition to the small number of schools which prove daily that youngsters can develop properly and become well educated without being pressured or required to learn any prescribed curriculum, there are a large number of home-schoolers throughout the United States and in many foreign countries who are also proving it. Their term for it is unschooling.

Unschooling is a term which was used by John Holt, the former leader and revered mentor of the homeschooling movement. I believe the term is a misnomer because it implies that no learning is taking place, when in actuality it is a term which identifies a specific method of learning. A better term for it would be Voluntary Learning.

Not all homeschoolers are unschoolers, but a sizable portion of them are. Homeschoolers consider unschooling to be one of a number of legitimate avenues home educators may use to educate their children; however there are many homeschoolers who adamantly believe that unschooling is the ideal way to educate children.

Unschoolers believe the desire to learn must come from within the child, and that what is to be learned and how it is to be learned are the child's choice entirely. The parent is a facilitator but not a decision maker in the process. There are countless examples of children who have received good educations using this method, and many are well documented in *Home Education Magazine* and *Growing Without Schooling*, which are the two most popular homeschooling publications in the United States.

ACADEMIC ACHIEVEMENT VERSUS WHOLE-PERSON LEARNING

Most people believe that academic achievement should be the main goal of students, and that the success of schools and educators should be determined by measuring the academic achievements of their students. Isn't the reputation of every school determined primarily by the academic achievements of its students? Is there a public school in the U.S. today that is not preoccupied with its students achieving academic excellence; or, in the very least, academic competence?

Using academic achievement as the chief criteria for determining how successful students are in school fails to ensure that schools are nurturing the development of the whole person. In fact, using academic achievement as the chief criteria for determining how successful students are in school can, and often does, ensure that the development of the whole person is being set aside, undermined or violated. This is because academic achievement and developing the whole person are very different goals.

To develop the whole person, the goal must be to develop all the significant parts of the person in synchronization with one another. The person's social skills, self-identity, awareness, reasoning skills, survival skills, moral and ethical judgment, emotional development, physical health and overall well being must be focused on simultaneously, and those parts that are found to be particularly lacking should receive special and immediate attention, insofar as possible.

Please note that, in the list just provided, there is no reference to academic achievement. That is because there is no part of the whole person which can be identified as the "academic achievement" part. One cannot focus on developing the "academic achievement" part of the whole person because there is no such part of the whole person. Consequently, if educators aim to develop the whole person, they should not channel the learner toward academic achievement because it misleads the learner and confuses the objective. While academic achievement can be a byproduct of developing the whole person, it can never be the aim if the development of the whole person is to be the focus.

If a marksman aims an arrow at one target, he cannot expect to hit a different one which is in another location. Similarly, when an educator aims the child toward academic excellence or academic competence, he cannot expect that the end result will be the enhanced development of the whole person.

The goals of <u>academic excellence or academic competence</u> and the development of the whole person are not only different from one another, but they are not even related. A person can be an academic wizard at the same time that he is an incompetent and poorly developed human being. For instance, a person can have a vast store of knowledge in a particular academic subject or be well-versed in several academic subjects, yet he may still reason poorly, have a poorly developed self-identity, have poor social skills, have poor ethical judgment, have poor survival skills, have poor observational skills, be poorly equipped to maneuver in his own environment, be emotionally immature and be unhappy and miserable to boot. Despite his academic achievements, would such a person be an asset to himself, other people or his community?

With these ideas in mind, it is appropriate to ask the following questions: Can the development of the whole person be an educational goal? Can it be the primary objective of a school for youth? And if it is the primary objective of a school for youth, how would that school function?

The second question is particularly important. The development of the whole person should be the central educational goal of every school for youth, especially of every school for children, because the developmental needs of children are critical, substantial and key to their current well being and future success and happiness. This is less true for older teenagers. To immerse children in educational programs which are not ultra sensitive (in thought and deed) to their developmental needs is to harm them because it foregoes giving their developmental needs the attention they deserve and require.

The developmental needs of children are of such overriding and all-encompassing importance to the current well being and future prosperity of children that there can be no legitimate or constructive education of children that is insensitive to, or in conflict with, those developmental needs. Therefore, one cannot aim for academic excellence or academic competence when educating children and simply assume that, in doing so, their developmental needs will thereby be sufficiently accommodated and reinforced. An enlightened educator will realize that preoccupation with academic competence or

154

academic excellence interferes with the developmental needs of children.

If academic achievement is not the central concern of schools for youth, and instead the central concern is the education of the whole person, can the school still be a school? In other words, can it adequately and properly educate youngsters? The answer is, unequivocally, yes. But the learning process itself is viewed differently and the methods used by educators are different than those used by traditional educators.

NATURAL LEARNING

Natural learning is the learning people do every day of their lives. It is usually taken for granted by educators. Most educators assume it will occur of its own accord regardless of whatever else happens in the person's life; and that, in any event, it is not their province or responsibility. However, natural learning is so vital to a person's growth and happiness that it should never be taken for granted by educators or by anyone concerned about the growth and development of people.

More than any other type of learning, natural learning determines a person's character, identity, values and morals, personality, thinking skills, living skills, overall perspective and overall development as a human being. Natural learning provides the foundation for all the other learning a person engages in, and thus is a vital part of it. Before academic learning (learning prescribed by a school or school teacher) was even conceived of, the people of the world were being educated by the process of natural learning. Natural learning is, and will always remain, the most important form of learning.

Natural learning differs from academic learning, and from other forms of mandated, required or prescribed learning, in that it is done solely to please the learner. It is not done to please teachers, employers, parents, society, friends, family or anyone other than the learner.

Natural learning is the learning people do <u>voluntarily</u> to satisfy their curiosity, to increase their awareness and understanding, to develop their skills and abilities, to grow and mature, or for personal gratification or personal fulfillment. Natural learning often occurs as a byproduct of simply living one's life, but it can also be the result of a conscious effort to learn.

Natural learning is invigorating because the learner feels a strong personal connection to what is being learned, is ripe for it and has selected it. Things that are learned naturally are overflowing with personal relevance and personal significance. .... Whereas other types of learning are often dead affairs which the learner is not committed to or interested in. There is often a revulsion connected with them because they did not occur out of choice. The connection between the learner and the things learned are often poor at best.

Natural learning is almost always in harmony with a

156

person's needs, wants, circumstances and natural inclinations. It occurs when a person is ready for it to occur, and not before. It is an extremely personal process in terms of its content, timing and method. It is idiosyncratic and unique for each person. It is of the person and for the person. It accommodates the person's self-development.

Natural learning is a very complex form of learning because it fits the person as well as a finely tailored suit or perfectly crafted dentures. It fits their mind, their personality, their developmental needs, their life-circumstances, their preferences, moods and inclinations. This type of learning cannot be supervised by anyone other than the learner because no one other than the learner can know what he needs to learn from day to day, or what method of learning would be most suitable to him.

Natural learning could consist of reading, observing, thinking, interacting, experiencing, reacting, initiating an activity, experimenting, expressing oneself and so forth. It could consist of going for a walk to contemplate an idea. It could consist of challenging a professor's thinking or an expert's opinions. It could consist of reading one page of a book and mulling over that page for one year before reading any more of the book. It may consist of thinking about your life and avoiding reading books altogether for five years, then reading voraciously every day for the next five years. Natural learning could consist of learning through extensive socializing with people, or through working at many different jobs, or through pursuing an unusual hobby with great zeal and intensity. There are so many ways in which to learn naturally that it would be foolish to attempt to identify all of them. One can learn naturally by getting in touch with their feelings, by learning to be more objective, or though developing a special relationship with a friend. All of these types of natural learning and many others weave themselves into a complex fabric which ends up making up the mind and emotions of a person, for better or worse.

Natural learning is a logical and synchronized progression of a person's thinking, feeling, skills, awareness, personality, identity, overall perspective, and overall relationship to the world around him. As an ice skater improves her stamina, muscular strength, agility, technical skills and mental attitude in a logical and synchronized progression from the simple and easy to the more complex and difficult, natural learning occurs

157

in a logical and synchronized progression from the simple and easy to the more complex and difficult.

The way a tree grows serves perfectly to describe the path of natural learning. Just as the trunk of a tree must precede the branches, and the lower branches must precede the upper branches, and the branches must precede the leaves, the natural learner cannot jump ahead of himself. His development as a whole person must occur in stages based upon his entire readiness, and efforts to focus unduly on certain aspects of his learning which the whole person cannot accommodate are foolish.

Natural learning requires appropriate conditions and circumstances to occur in an optimal way. If professional educators are going to be concerned with the development of the whole person, one of their jobs should be to determine what those optimal conditions and circumstances are.

Natural learning can be thwarted, blocked or undermined. If professional educators are going to be concerned with the development of the whole person, one of their jobs should be to determine how and when natural learning is thwarted, blocked or undermined.

Just as a person cannot be in different places at the same time, the human mind commonly cannot attend adequately to both the natural learning it needs to be doing and the academic learning required by professional educators. When there is a conflict between the natural learning people need to be doing and the academic learning required by educators, the educator concerned about the development of the whole person will favor the natural learning that needs to be done.

Even though academic learning has an important role in the education of adults, it should not occur at the expense of their natural learning. Do to their extensive and acute developmental needs, the academic learning that children do should be entirely optional and voluntary. The best way to educate youngsters is by making sure all the learning they do is synchronized with their developmental needs. This means that youngsters should be permitted to learn naturally, both inside of school and outside of it. Learning should be their friend, not their adversary.

VOLUNTARY EDUCATION

There is an alternative to the frustration, pain and disappointment of traditional schools and traditional teaching methods. It's called Voluntary Education. Voluntary Education is the reverse of compulsory education, both in idea and method. Voluntary Education seeks to develop the whole person. Academic excellence is not its focus or objective, although it may be its byproduct. Voluntary Education is concerned with learning as a process, not as an outcome; therefore, grading or testing the voluntary learner is inappropriate.

Grading and testing are inappropriate for the voluntary learner because one of their primary uses is to control the content and outcome of the learning people do. No one can learn voluntarily when the content and outcome of their learning are determined by others. Non-intrusive techniques of evaluation that are not used to control, manipulate, mandate or prescribe the content or outcome of learning, but are voluntarily agreed to by students and used solely to aid students, educators and parents in understanding the progress of the learner, do not violate the spirit or intent of voluntary learning, and should therefore be permitted.

Voluntary Education can be used to educate children or adults, although the rationale for its use in educating children differs somewhat from the rationale for its use in educating adults. Voluntary Education for children proceeds from the idea that it is much more important for the whole child to develop properly than to achieve academic excellence. Striving for academic excellence distracts both teacher and child from the goal of educating the whole child and interferes with the child's development in many important ways.

Suppose it is a child's destiny to become an artist. Things having to do with his destiny will call out to him. It could be a tree, birds, colors, no one knows. Not even the child knows. Yet, a fragile something within him knows, and in mysterious ways it prepares the child for its future. Now, what happens when the big, bad and overpowering superstructure called Compulsory or Formal education swoops down on the child with an array of assignments, tests, homework, and extensive rules for behavior in school, including guidelines for focusing attention in the classroom? A logical person must conclude that the natural inclinations of the child are opposed, interfered with, under-

159

mined, even uprooted as a consequence. That is unethical and clearly immoral, for it is denying a youngster the right, the privilege, to be true to nature's plan for him or her.

Voluntary Education relies on two assumptions:

(1) The impulse to learn is inborn in very child, and will become activated (if it isn't already) when given the proper learning environment.

(2) The desire to improve oneself and become a competent and worthwhile human being is a natural characteristic of people that will blossom when given the proper learning environment.

These two assumptions preempt the need for compulsory or required learning. If the two assumptions are valid, there is no need for required curricula when educating youth.

Due to the fact that the mind of the child is fragile, vulnerable and susceptible, it must never be controlled by educators. Instead it should be set free to find its own direction and pattern of development. Educational resources and opportunities can be provided to children, but they should never be imposed on them. The learning that children do can be stimulated, encouraged and assisted by educators, but it should never be required or mandated.

If Voluntary Education for children is not graded or tested, one might wonder how it can be evaluated to determine its usefulness and effectiveness. There are a multitude of ways to evaluate the voluntary learner. One way is by the product he or she voluntarily produces. Seldom does a person do nothing. Children are very active, and their activity will produce a product. Given an educational environment rich in learning resources and opportunities, and presided over by qualified educators, the voluntary learning that children do will be rich with learning product that educators can evaluate in as many different ways as their imaginations can discover. Another way of evaluating the voluntary learner is by determining his or her progress as a whole person. Such questions can be asked as: Is the child developing social skills at school? Is the child developing an identity of his own or does he rely too much on others in determining his wants and interests? Is the child becoming more independent, both in his learning habits and other life-tasks? Does the child benefit from being in school? Does the child enjoy his school? What interests does the child have, and are they being properly encouraged and assisted by educators?

Voluntary Education caters to and accommodates the mental make-up and natural response patterns of the learner. What is taught and how it is taught is less important than how the learner is responding to it. The responses of the learner dictate the direction and content of the teaching. A voluntary learner understands that he or she need not be receptive to a teacher's offerings or suggestions; consequently, the usefulness of the teacher is determined by the student's receptivity to the teacher.

SOME CHARACTERISTICS OF
VOLUNTARY LEARNING

The Voluntary Learner learns because he or she wants to, not in order to satisfy the demands, requirements or expectations of educators. The traditional educator may claim that her students are learning from her because they want to, but often it is a false assumption or wishful thinking. It is true that when the traditional teacher has great luck, and her expectations of her students and the students' learning inclinations are in excellent harmony, both the will of the teacher and the learning desires of her students may mesh beautifully, but more often there is a serious discrepancy between what a teacher expects of her students and their learning interests and inclinations.

Even subtle differences between a student's learning interests and inclinations *and* a teacher's expectations and requirements can seriously disrupt a student's progress and sense of well being. For instance, imagine a class of Kindergarten or early elementary children, in which the teacher has allocated a period for painting. One of the children has a yen to experiment with colors, and is dabbing paint on a sheet of paper in what appears to be a nonsensical pattern but she is having fun. Since the teacher has been taught that the objective of art should be recognizable forms, she interrupts the child's experimenting to suggest that she draw something practical, like a tree, ball or boat, or even water or grass.

While the teacher, who has thus intervened in the creativity of the child, may be a caring, good and kind person, her action may not only have disrupted the creativity of the child, but may have seriously tampered with the child's individuality, freedom of expression, and possibly with the child's ultimate potential as a human being.

It is thousands upon thousands of subtle creative urges and subtle learning impulses, and more powerful creative outbursts and inspirations which – added together – make a great painter, thinker or just a great human being. When the teacher begins intervening in the natural learning impulses and urges of early youth, and replaces those with her will, she is denying the child the right to evolve naturally. She is bending the creative processes of the child to her will, and adapting the learning inclinations, urges and impulses of the child to her plan or program. In doing so, she not only transforms them, but distorts and aborts them. They are no longer the child's, or even of the child. They are now of the teacher and for the teacher. The child learns that both learning and creating, to be approved of, must be an extension of the teacher's expectations. This is what traditional educators call learning. The result is a tragedy of untold proportions.

Teachers of children all over the world who have told children that they cannot merely dab paints or draw strange forms may well be destroying our artists of the future; but worse, they are tampering with the inner happiness and natural growth patterns of young learners. Would you want to become a painter if someone told you that you could *not* paint abstract forms, or hold a brush in a certain way, or put paint on your paper in thick globs because it wasted paint and was not pretty – even though these are the things you wanted to do and felt comfortable doing? Can you see that such interference from a person who had authority over you might discourage your efforts altogether and dampen your interest not only in art, but in being yourself?

This is why many students hate their schools. (Please see the Second Introduction of this book, within the section entitled Student Unrest, for examples of students who hate their schools). They feel tampered with, interfered with and controlled by educators. They sense the walls of a prison closing in on them, and they see teachers as wardens of that prison. They are not wrong. They have correctly identified their school experience. It is the schools that have erred, and teachers, and curriculum designers, and Boards of Education, and Superintendents of Schools. They have erred because they have not understood that learning is a creative and individual process intimately connected with the development of each child, and because they have not understood that the learning children do belongs to them. The learning process, content and outcome all belong to the children; not to professional educators. Professional educators have no right to intercede in the process, content or outcome of children's learning in order to make it their own (belonging to educators); for, in doing so, they steal the native and natural learning experiences of children away from them and replace them with artificial learning experiences which they have designed. These educators are thieves of childrens' creativity, identity and natural development.

163

TEACHING THINKING SKILLS TO ADULTS

We all know that the traditional role of the teacher is that of a person who imparts knowledge, and that educators as well as society would usually give any teacher high marks who successfully imparts useful knowledge to students. But imparting knowledge is not the same as nurturing thinking skills. Just because a student has acquired a collection of useful facts and information does not mean he or she is a skilled or effective thinker, able to put the facts and information to good use. Consequently, I do not believe a teacher of adults should be deemed successful unless he or she has not only aided students in acquiring knowledge, but also nurtured thinking skills in the process.

There must be many ways to nurture thinking skills, but there is one way which cries out for recognition. It concerns the ability to form opinions and make decisions. If a person is not highly skilled at forming opinions and making decisions, no amount of knowledge will enable him or her to be a proficient or skilled thinker.

The ability to form opinions and make decisions, which is perhaps the most important of all thinking skills, cannot be acquired by learning to mimic or parrot the ideas of others. It can only be acquired by developing the habit of diverging from the ideas of others and pursuing innovative and even unpopular avenues of speculation, and learning to rely on one's own thinking. Yet, in today's schools, when teachers impart knowledge, they usually expect students to accept it or agree to it. If a student does not accept or agree to what the teacher is offering, wouldn't immersing oneself in it, and memorizing it, be offensive and unpalatable? So there is an assumption on the part of both teachers and schools that contained in the act of immersing oneself in, and memorizing, the information, facts and ideas they offer is a tacit acceptance of what they are offering. The whole process of immersion and memorization without dissent – which is the primary method of educating people in today's schools – does not encourage the ability to form opinions and make decisions, and that is a serious if not fatal flaw.

To correct this problem, divergence, dissent and self-reliance must be encouraged in all aspects of the educational process.

The education of adults should not favor immersion and memorization of what teachers and schools offer at the expense of divergence, dissent and self-reliance. To facilitate divergence, dissent and self-reliance within all aspects of adult education, and thus nurture the ability to form opinions and make decisions, I recommend the following procedure be implemented, insofar as possible, within all courses of instruction: Dividing the course of instruction into two equal parts, the first consisting of surveying and acquiring relevant and useful information; and the second consisting of relying on one's own initiative to diverge from that information, disagree with it, and pursue alternatives to it.

Thus, a college course in Psychology, for example, could be divided into two equal parts in the semester in which it is offered. The first part would be to survey and learn pertinent information, and the second would consist of giving the students complete freedom to diverge from, oppose, and formulate alternatives to, what has just been learned. If the course being taught is a course on the thinking of prominent figures in psychology, such as William James, Sigmund Freud, Abraham Maslow and others, the first half of the course would consist of surveying and familiarizing oneself with their ideas, and perhaps being tested for one's newly acquired knowledge; and the second half would consist of opposing their ideas, diverging from them and thinking of alternatives to them. The teacher could begin the second half of the course by asking the students such questions as: "In what ways do you believe the thinking of Freud, or any of the others whose ideas we have studied is flawed or incorrect, and what alternatives to their thinking and practices would you propose?" "In what ways is the teaching of this course faulty or unappealing to you, and what different subject matter or methods of instruction would you propose?"

Questions such as the preceding ones can greatly enliven every course of instruction by placing more emphasis on the opinions, reactions and choices of students; and by avoiding the mere regurgitation of ideas, which stagnates the learning process as well as entire fields of study.

TWO CHOICES

Since most teachers of school-age youngsters (ages 5-17 in the U.S.) currently earn their living working in a compulsory system of education (compulsory not only because attendance is required, but also because an assigned curriculum is imposed), it may seem to them pointless to contemplate or advocate a radically different, or opposing, system of education that would never be sanctioned by administrators of the system in which they teach. However, in order to bring honor to their profession, I believe educators have a duty to consider, advocate; and, insofar as they are permitted, experiment with, any system of education which seems to them promising, even though it may be radically different from, or at odds with, the system in which they teach. How else can needed improvements be fostered? With these ideas in mind, I would now like to compare the two very different alternatives to educating youngsters I have been focusing on in this book: Compulsory Education and Voluntary Education.

In a compulsory system of education, force is used by educators, either overtly or subtly, as a means of implementing their objectives. Youngsters are pressured to learn an assigned curriculum. Little faith is placed in the student's native desire to learn. Little faith is placed in the student's ability to discover a beneficial path of learning and development for himself. Little respect is given to the uniqueness of the individual student, or to his right of self-governing, or to the wisdom of his personal choices. It should not surprise anyone that large numbers of young people instinctively rebel against this approach to educating them, and are offended and insulted by it.

In a system of Voluntary Education, the uniqueness of the individual is respected, as are his or her personal choices. Great faith is placed in the individual learner's ability to discover, in his own way and at his own pace, a beneficial and suitable path of learning and development. All the ingredients of the learning environment, as well as the efforts of the teachers, are aimed at empowering the student to take responsibility for his or her own learning and development. In this environment, teachers do not demand or require learning from their students. All learning is the choice of the student. In this system of education, an environment that is rich in learning resources and opportunities is provided to youngsters. This environment

166

comes with instructors who are knowledgeable in their respective fields, who are skilled in communicating with, and in relating to, young people, and who can inspire the trust and confidence of young people. Their purpose is assisting students in discovering their own path of learning and facilitating students' learning efforts. This system caters to the learning habits, interests and inclinations of the individual student. The student is expected to be responsible for, and to discover, his or her own path of learning. The beauty of this approach is that it permits a youngster's education to be integrated with his overall development and to be an outgrowth of it.

To many educators trained in traditional methods of teaching, Voluntary Education will appear to be ludicrous. However, large numbers of homeschoolers around the world are becoming knowledgeable about the wisdom, effectiveness and methodology of this approach, and traditional educators need to catch up. At a homeschooling conference I attended in Long Beach, California in 1996, much of the talk was on the primacy of learner-led learning as a method of educating youngsters. Learner-led learning is the opposite of teacher-led learning, both in idea and method. The teacher follows the lead of the learner, who does not necessarily require, or want, the assistance of the teacher in order to learn. The needs and interests of the learner determine when, and what, the teacher will teach. Many people who advocate learner-led learning, myself included, do not view the two approaches as being compatible with one another.

The idea that teacher-led learning is the only way to accomplish effective instruction of youth is so ingrained in the consciousness of humankind that learner-led learning is a concept difficult to grasp – until one realizes that, for the human being, learning comes as naturally as breathing. If given a friendly learning environment, rich in learning resources and opportunities and presided over by enlightened and capable learning facilitators, youngsters will be eager to learn voluntarily. It is important to note that a teacher can play a very active role in teaching voluntary learners, but she must be voluntarily accessed by them. The teacher may even lecture or give assignments, but these must be voluntarily accessed by students who are not required or expected to do so.

It is time for all traditional educators to realize that there is another way to educate youngsters which is very useful and effective, which is very promising and worthwhile; and which just happens to be the opposite of Compulsory Education, both in concept and practice. Educators who are open minded will give Voluntary Education a chance to prove itself, using its own methods, unimpeded by the terms, rules, regulations or practices of Compulsory Education. Voluntary Education for youth deserves and requires its own schools, publicly as well as privately funded, and its own brand of teachers; and must make its own rules, without the interference of any government or state entity. If given a chance to become established and to operate unimpeded, publicly and privately funded schools of Voluntary Learning for youth will prove themselves to be of great benefit to the well being, happiness and proper development of youth. They will also prove themselves to be essential to our Democracy because a society cannot be truly free, nor a Democracy truly Democratic, until its children learn in an atmosphere based on freedom and trust, rather than on submission and obedience.

Ordering Information

The following books of philosophy by Ron Dultz can now be ordered directly from the author:

1. *Educating the Entire Person* $10
2. *A New Approach to Human Psychology* $10
(Price includes free shipping. All orders promptly shipped.)

To order, please send payment along with your return address to: Ron Dultz; P.O. Box 370985; Reseda, CA 91337.

Please inquire about reduced prices for bulk orders.

Correspondence

Your correspondence is invited, and will be answered. Please direct your correspondence to the author at the above address.